JUST
another
GOODBYE

DR SHARON ZAFFARESE-DIPPOLD

 ZeeT Publishing

Dear Reader-

Thank you for purchasing my life story. My goal in sharing my life with you is to bring about awareness and promote change in the foster care system.

The names and locations in this book have been changed to maintain the privacy of others.

Just Another Goodbye, the third part of the Garbage Bag Life series, has been written to depict language and thought processes that are reminiscent of a nine-year-old child living in an abusive environment.

Mild language was also used to accurately illustrate Dr. Sharon Zaffarese-Dippold's home life.

The young lady photographed for the book's cover is a model and not the child narrator in the book.

A percentage of all net book sales is being donated to "**His Tabernacle Family Church in Ithaca New York. (Embrace Grace Program)**

A percentage of all net book sales is being donated to The "Ticket to Dream" National Foster Care Foundation.

The past does not define us. *You* define you.

And for those of us who lived in or do live in foster care… we are worth more than garbage bags.

With deep appreciation and gratitude:
~ Dr. Sharon Zaffarese-Dippold

Books in the Garbage Bag Life Series
by Dr. Sharon Zaffarese-Dippold Ph.D.,
LCSWR, LCSW, CCTP

Just Another Slice
Just Another Raggedy Doll
Just Another Goodbye
Just Another Hiding Place

Content/Trigger Warning

This book contains content related to physical abuse of a child and mild language.

I hope this book brings awareness about Post Traumatic Stress Disorder and Domestic Violence. All parents should have a conversation regarding abuse with their children, regardless of them being foster children.

If needed, the following numbers are for emotional support and guidance.

- ❖ National Suicide Hotline Number- ❖ 1-800-273-8255
- ❖ SAMHSA National Helpline for Mental Health- 1-800-662-HELP (4357)
- ❖ SAMHSA National Helpline for Substance Use- 1-800-662-HELP (4357)
- ❖ Mental Health- 211 (You can call this number for Mental Health assistance for yourself or if you are worried about someone else.)
- ❖ 911- If you feel you are in a state of emergency, please call and someone will help you immediately.
- ❖ 988 Suicide Hotline
- ❖ National Domestic Violence Hotline 1-800-799-7233 or SMS-Text START to 88788

As an author, my goal in sharing my true story with you about my lived experience in foster care is that of motivation and encouragement. At the same time, please reach out for assistance if needed and stay safe.

The past does not make you.
You make you

Gifts I've Received

My Children
Jessica & Jason Tubbs
Joseph & Elizabeth Zaffarese

My Grandchildren
Zeta
Enoch
Elijah
Tiberius

A percentage of all net sales are being donated to

Why duffel bags are important:

There are over 400,000 children in foster care and one child enters care every two minutes. They enter foster care through no fault of their own and with very little notice. When removed from their homes, too often a few personal belongings are shoved in a trash bag that follows that child to their placement. By providing children with duffel bags as they enter care or move homes, we are providing them with dignity and a small piece of comfort during a scary time.

Why aging-out support is important:

Every year 20,000 youth age-out of foster care. Facing instant adulthood, they must independently find housing and employment, often without a high school diploma or job experience. With no support system in place, young adults exiting foster care are often one minor emergency away from homelessness.

Ticket to Dream works to provide support and resources that help improve graduation rates, increase college acceptance, provide job training, teach valuable life skills, provide access to technology, and ensure these young adults have safe and reliable housing. It is a nationwide organization that aims to fill the unmet needs of children experiencing foster and kinship care. We work with a nationwide network of supporters, corporations, and nonprofits to boost self-worth, reduce future homelessness, reduce trauma upon entry into care, help them reach their future goals, and provide opportunities to experience childhood. To date, Ticket to Dream has reached over 4 million children in the foster care system. You can learn more at tickettodream.org or follow us on social @tickettodream.

Ticket to Dream provides access to duffel bags to help ease the transition to a new home. Our 1st Night Kits were created to help the community give back to children entering foster care while also providing comfort items that can bring relief during a scary time. Armed with a 1st Night Kit, we also eliminate the need for foster parents to rush to the store at the last minute to fulfill unmet needs. Additionally, we put an emphasis on collecting and providing backpacks to foster youth during the back to school season knowing that a quality backpack can boost self-esteem during the school year while also doubling as luggage when needed.

Preface

When does a person reach the point where it doesn't matter where they go? When will I become numb to this fear that makes every part of my body shake? Shouldn't this be normal for Curtis and me?

Ain't sitting in this ugly car with Mrs. Alex looking at us in her rearview mirror something I should be used to?

How many times have I looked at her face in that tiny, little mirror? How many times?

Is this going to be my life from now on? One car ride to another? One goodbye to another?

At what point will my heart stop hurting?

At what point will someone want me?

Chapter 1
Little Mirror

"Anna, where're we going?" My little brother croaks out like a frog.

"I don't know, Curtis. I'm sure Mrs. Alex is taking us to a new family."

"I don't want a new family. I want to go back to Mom." He wipes his nose on his bare arm. "I want to go back to Mom!" He shoves the garbage bags to the floor.

They hit the back of Mrs. Alex's seat as he leans his head against the car window and tries to catch his breath.

Why is he not sitting next to me like he always does? I stare at Curtis who's now making circles on the window with his finger.

"Anyone hungry?"

And there it is, the question Mrs. Alex always asks us on our car rides to the unknown.

"No! We're not hungry!" Curtis yells this before I can answer.

Wow. That's so not like him. He never yells at adults, and especially not at Mrs. Alex.

"Curtis was that you, my dear boy? You are *not* to talk to me that way. I expect it from your sister, but not from you."

Of course *I'm* the bad one, though, I guess it *is* usually me on these rides who's yelling at Mrs. Alex.

"Well, I'm going to stop anyway because I'm hungry. If you two are going to change your minds, you have time to decide."

Really? She's going to feed her face after she just ripped us from another family?

Mrs. Alex starts singing a song about country roads, taking her home. Her squeaky voice piercing my eardrums irritates me as much as the sad memory of Daddy who used to sing this song to me all the time when we worked in the garage.

"Stop singing, you're hurting my ears." I say it almost as loudly as Curtis did.

She ignores me. "We're here. Who's going into the restaurant with me to get something to eat?"

I look out the car window.

"Well, are you two going to sit there and say nothing?"

Finally, Mrs. Alex gets something right.

Slam! She slams her door.

"Anna, I'm not hungry," Curtis grabs my hand.

"Me neither," I mumble.

We stare at her through the window as she stands by the car as if she thinks we will change our minds.

We won't.

She waves, then heads into the fast-food place, like always.

Mrs. Alex *always* disappears. She's too good at leaving us behind. Like we are nothing and don't mean anything to her.

The leather under us crunches as Curtis moves closer to me in the back seat. "I'm scared, Anna. What if this family is like our first mother? What if this family has mean, older brothers? What if this family... doesn't like me?"

I wrap my arm around his shoulder and pull him close to me. "How

2

can they not like you, Curtis? You're the smart one. You get good grades. And you—"

"And I'm mad. I didn't want to leave. Mom was the best Mom ever. Way better than Mother was, and now I have to have a new one. I don't want a new one." He wipes his eyes with his fingers as his tears multiply.

"Why, Anna? She was so nice to us. Why did that damn fire have to happen anyway? Why?" Curtis kicks the back of Mrs. Alex's seat and crosses his arms in front of him. If she would have been sitting in it, he could have pushed her through the windshield.

"I don't know Curtis. Maybe she really didn't have a place for us to sle—"

"Bullshit, Anna! That's crap."

Now Curtis sounds like my old foster brothers in my first foster home. I've never seen him this mad. I've seen him scared, but not mad like this.

Wham! Wham! He punches the back of Mrs. Alex's seat with his fist. "Take me back! Take me back now!" *Wham! Wham*! He punches the seat some more.

I'm not sure what more he's going to do. What if he punches the window and hurts himself?

My stomach aches which always happens when I'm nervous. I don't know what to do to calm him down. I don't—

Someone taps the window.

I jerk my head and see a little old lady standing next to the car. I roll my window down a little because I can tell she's talking, but I can't hear her.

"Are you okay in there, dear?" She points to Curtis on the other side of the seat. "Is he okay? I can hear him screaming across the parking lot and I wanted to check on you."

I bring my hand up and wiggle my fingers. "We're okay. My brother's just ma—"

"You're damn right I'm mad." Curtis kicks the back of the seat yet again. "We're foster kids and no one wants us, so if you know what's good for you, you'll leave us alone cuz we must have cooties or something because everyone keeps giving us away."

The lady backs away from the car. "Oh dear." She covers her mouth with her hand.

That's what Mom used to do when she was surprised by something.

Curtis kicks Mrs. Alex's seat some more and grunts like he's trying to move the entire car with his legs.

"Honey, do you want me to get help? Is your mother inside the restaurant?" She points at the building.

Did she *not* just hear him? "No, our mother isn't in that building, but our caseworker is because we're foster kids."

She leans close. "You're foster kids?" she whispers like she just heard a dirty little secret.

Are we a dirty secret? Curtis and I... kids no one wants.

Are we dirty?

"We're okay. Thanks for checking on us." I roll my window back up and hope this old lady leaves us alone.

It works. I watch her walk to her yellow car.

I sit hugging my doll while I watch Curtis hug himself with his arms.

For a moment, I close my eyes and there is nothing—no noise, no crying, no talking, and no fear. It's just nothing.

I sit in the silence a little more as my doll's hair tickles my nose. That is... 'til Mrs. Alex's scratchy voice interrupts my momentary peace. "Yum. You kids don't know what you missed." The car door slams behind her, jarring me out of my thoughts. "You should never pass up fast food when you get a chance." She licks her fingers, smiling at me in the little mirror. "Anna, would you like to say something?"

"Yeah—your lipstick's all over your mouth." I hadn't planned to say anything at first, but her smile made my anger boil—like the water Mom would put in a pot on the stove to make spaghetti.

". Anna's right." Curtis points at the mirror. "You have lipstick all over your face." He laughs some more. He laughs, thankfully. I'd rather see him laughing than as mad as he was. I think he would have hurt Mrs. Alex if she'd been in the car.

"That's enough out of both of you!" She wipes off the lipstick with a tissue. "Now, buckle up. This next fam—"

"I don't want to hear about the next family," Curtis says, his voice rising in pitch. "I want you to take me back to my mom."

"Honey, I'm sorry but that's not possible. Sue and Allen no longer have a bedroom for you to sleep in. To be foster parents, they have to make sure you have a bedroom. Plus, Mrs. Stone felt that she couldn't take care of you after the fire."

"Bullshit!" he screams.

"Curtis! Where did you learn that word?" Mrs. Alex whips her head around so fast I think it's going to come off her shoulders. Her beady eyes stare at my brother.

"From my old mother with the Connors. Where the hell do you think I learned it from? Huh?" Curtis's face turns red. "You think you're so smart. Why didn't you know that, huh?" He keeps repeating the same word "huh" again and again.

Someone must have glued my butt to the seat. I have no words, and I'm not sure what to do. I've never seen him like this. I've never seen him this mad. I don't even know this kid next to me. I know he *looks* like Curtis, but he acts like an alien who's taken over his body. I want to shake the alien and tell him to leave my brother's body. I want Curtis back. But no way am I going to try to touch him right now.

He raises a fist up and—

Bam! Mrs. Alex slams forward and hits the steering wheel.

"Hold on kids!" She steers the car in one direction and then another.

Curtis slides onto my lap on top of my doll and I'm thrown against the door handle.

Stones hit the side of the car as we fly off the road into the dirt.

The car jerks to a stop.

I don't move and neither does Curtis.

"Great. Just great." Mrs. Alex gets out of the car.

"Curtis?" I whisper. For the first time in my life, I'm honestly worried about what he will do next.

"What?"

I take a deep breath. Thank goodness, it sounds like he's back. "Are you okay? You went flying across the seat when you hit me."

Curtis crawls out of my lap, rubbing his arm as if he has a Charlie horse. "Yeah. I'm okay. Did I do this? Did I cause us to wreck?" His eyes grow round as Mrs. Alex walks around to the back of the car.

"Nope. Mrs. Alex is just a horrible driver." We both giggle.

I do, however, think we wrecked because he *did* punch the back of her seat. But I'm not telling him that because I don't want the alien to come back.

The car door creaks open, then Mrs. Alex gets into the driver's seat. She looks in the little mirror. "See what you did?" She points to Curtis.

That's it! She will *not* make the alien come back. I won't let her.

"It isn't *his* fault; it's *yours*, because you're a horrible driver. Don't you dare blame my brother." I point right back at her in that little mirror. My doll drops to the floor as I slide to the edge of the back seat to get closer to the front.

Mrs. Alex's eyes get big as she looks at me and then Curtis. I turn to see what she's staring at.

My brother's face is purple.

I can see all the veins in his forehead, down the side of his face, and in his neck. I swear his head is going to explode like a bomb.

"Curtis, are you okay?"

He doesn't answer me.

"Curtis! Curtis, are you okay?"

He turns away from Mrs. Alex and locks eyes with me.

I hear his teeth grinding.

With his lips shut, he mumbles, "I'm *fine.*"

Mrs. Alex doesn't say another word and starts the car.

Curtis leans in and whispers, "Anna, if she looks at me one more time in that tiny mirror, she's going to eat my sneaker." The blood vessels in his forehead pop out.

He's not joking.

"Don't let that witch get to you." I hope my words change his mind.

He growls like a dog under his breath as he leans against the car window.

For the first time, Curtis scares me. Not because I think he is going to hurt me, but because I think he seriously wants to hurt Mrs. Alex.

Please don't look at us in the mirror. Please.

This car ride seems to take longer than it did when we'd gone to our previous foster home. I squeeze my doll as Curtis calms down and falls asleep. I have no clue where we are, and all I see are big houses and lots of farms.

The car slows.

"Well, kids, here we are.." She looks in the little mirror.

I'm so glad Curtis didn't hear her because she might've had to eat his shoe. And while I wouldn't mind her feeling bad like we do, I don't want Curtis to get in trouble.

"Let's get you inside." Mrs. Alex sounds happy.

Probably because she's gonna get rid of us, but there's nothing happy about any of this. There's nothing happy about going to a home that you don't know or living with strangers. There's nothing happy about carrying everything you own in a trash bag. I want to scream at her smirky, blood-red, smiling lips.

But I don't. Because it doesn't matter if I scream. This is where I hafta go.

I squint through the window. Though it's dark outside, this house is lit up like the Christmas tree at our old families' houses. There are tall poles everywhere with lights on.

And I see something here that might make this, well, if not happy, at least not so bad.

Chapter 2
Bean Bag Chairs

There's a barn. *A barn.* Maybe they have a horse. While no horse will ever replace my Thunder, it'd be nice to have another friend I can ride to get away from everything bad.

If only I were sitting on Thunder instead of in this stinky car...

Mrs. Alex pulls the car into a little, covered tent where three other vehicles are parked...

I nudge Curtis.

"Curtis," I whisper and push his leg harder. "Curtis."

He lifts his head.

"We're here."

"*Here*? Where's here?" My brother wipes his eyes.

I'm confused and don't understand his question. He knows we are going to a new family, so why did he ask where *here* is?

Curtis's eyes widen. "Oh, the new family. Anna, I don't like this. I don't want to be here." He scooches closer to me.

Mrs. Alex opens his car door. "About time you woke up." She points at Curtis. "I got these bags, and you can pick them up when you both get out of the car." Mrs. Alex grunts as she tries to lift the stuffed garbage bags. Sue and Allen had bought us a lot of stuff.

Curtis wraps his arm around me as Mrs. Alex fights with the garbage bags. "I don't want to be here. I don't want to do this." He tugs hard on my arm.

I want to yell at him that I don't want to do this either. I, too, don't want to move into this big, white house with black shutters. Even the big plants hanging all over the front porch, running the full length of the house, don't help me feel better. I don't want to be here.

Telling him that won't help though. "Look how nice the house looks, Curtis." I point out the window.

This doesn't stop Curtis from trying to pull me to the opposite side of the car when my door opens.

"Well, you two, let's get moving. As soon as I'm done with you, I have to move someone else." She waves at us.

Does she think this will move us? Well, it doesn't.

I smell fresh-cut grass. I love that smell. I take a big sniff. There is something else, another smell, that helps my belly feel better. Can it be? I sniff again. *Hay*. I smell hay. Like the bales of hay Thunder had in his stall in my last house.

Thunder. Oh, how I miss him.

"Come on, get out." Mrs. Alex's voice is sharp, like broken glass.

"Let's do this, Curtis." I grab my brother's hand and pull him out of the nasty car.

Before long, we are standing by our garbage bags again.

I hold my doll in one hand and drop Curtis's hand to grab the bags.

"No, Anna." My brother reaches for my hand again.

"Curtis, I hafta grab our garbage."

He raises his eyebrows. "You have to grab our *garbage*?"

I tilt my head. My brother's gaze doesn't move from mine. For a second, we don't talk. Then it hits me.

9

"Oh. Yeah. I hafta grab our garbage *bags*." Funny that I called our stuff *garbage*, but isn't that what it really is? Isn't that what *we* are?

I grunt as I drag the bags across the stones to the enormous front porch and clunk up the steps, each one feeling the weight of these heavy bags.

I want to throw up, standing at this front door, holding my doll and two garbage bags with Curtis behind me, holding onto my shirt. Is he crying again? He better stop—this family won't want a bunch of crybabies.

Mrs. Alex blocks my view as the door opens.

"Hello, Mrs. Alex," a woman says. "Come in. We've been waiting for you."

"I apologize. We couldn't get Anna into the car at the old house, so, it took most of the day to get her moving along. Then we couldn't get her off the horse next door. And, now, the kids didn't want to get out of the car, so I apologize for our lateness."

Of *course* she tells them it's my fault. How about it's *her* fault because she wanted to stop and get something to eat. It's her fault, not mine.

The garbage bags scrape against the doorway as I walk into a giant room with a big light hanging from the ceiling. I stare at the long white banister that goes all the way to the top of the stairs and down the hallway on the second floor.

"Wow. Those stairs are huge," Curtis mumbles behind me.

I hafta agree with him, and I can't wait to slide down that thing.

"Let me get your bags." A man emerges from another room and walks toward Mrs. Alex.

"Thanks, Jason. That would be nice."

Mrs. Alex is using her nice voice—one Curtis and I never hear.

My plan to escape this place is crushed by the sight of the tall man with dark hair barging into the room with us.

"Hello, kids." He nods at Mrs. Alex. "My name's Jason. You can call me whatever you like except, *Hey, man*." His eyes crinkle together as he smiles with tons of straight teeth.

I feel like the front door just swung closed and knocked me out because I can only see this man's face. Daddy? This man looks just like Daddy. He even has sideburns like Daddy.

"Hey, little girl. Those bags seem quite heavy for someone so small. Can I help you with them?" He reaches for the bags.

Small? *Little*? He thinks *I'm* small and little? I'll show him.

I back away fast and pull the garbage bags further behind me.

"Okay, okay. I get it. Those are your bags, and you want to be the one to carry them. But do you see those stairs and that long hallway?" He points at the huge staircase. "Your rooms are at the end of it. I'd prefer not to scratch the stairs with your bags banging on each step because Jessica would not be happy about that. So, either we leave your bags here, and you can carry the stuff out of them and walk everything one at a time up to your rooms, or I can carry the bags up the stairs to your rooms for you. Which one would you prefer?"

Jason sounds nice, but I will show him that I am not small or little. "I'll do it myself for my brother and me," I say sternly like Daddy taught me.

"Okay then." I turn and follow his gaze as it settles on our stuff. "We can leave those bags right here by the stairs. When Mrs. Alex is done, you and your brother can empty the bags and carry your stuff to your rooms." He smiles, and... winks?

My heart has butterflies going crazy in my belly. Even Jason's wink reminds me of Daddy. *I love you, Daddy, and I wish you were here with me.*

After I drop our bags, we follow Mrs. Alex and Jason through a big orange room with white trim making big squares all over the wall.

I run into the back of Mrs. Alex. "Ouch, kiddo, watch where you're walking."

"Don't stop walking so quickly, and I won't run into you!" I scream as I kick her leg, and keep doing it over and over 'til she falls.

"Do either of you play piano?"

I come out of my angry mind while Mrs. Alex stands next to a big instrument. My mind did it again. It pretends I am doing all kinds of things to people when I'm mad that I'm not actually doing.

"No. We don't play anything."

"What about the guy behind you? Do you play anything, big guy?"

Curtis says nothing and steps further behind me.

"No, my brother doesn't play any instruments either," I answer for him, just like in the old days. It's weird now. My brother is back to being his old self like he was before we moved in with Sue and Allen.

My strong brother, who never stopped talking and laughed all the time at the Stones' house, is gone. My heart hurts for him. I know he doesn't want to be here. I know he loved Sue. I also know that it's my fault we had to leave because I told Sue I didn't want to do secret girl time with her anymore. It's my fault my brother is sad.

Soon, we leave the orange piano room and go into another room that looks like the color of grapes. Boy, this family sure does like different colors.

"Would you like some tea, Mrs. Alexander?" The woman with the quiet voice from the front door comes into the grape room and sits with Jason.

"No, thank you, Jessica. I'm good." Mrs. Alex speaks in her disgustingly sweet, fake voice again.

"Hello, kids. My name is Jessica. I'm your new foster mom. I'm so glad to have you live with us. What kinds of things do you like to do?" She looks at me with eyes that are light green. She really is a pretty woman, and she looks way younger than Mrs. Alex because she doesn't have any wrinkles on her face.

"I'd like to take a minute as I need to give you all the details about these kids and the family they come from." Mrs. Alex bends down and clicks the button on her black bag to open it.

"Kids, why don't you sit on the sofa? There is plenty of room." Jasons pushed-together eyes stare at Mrs. Alex like he's trying to see something small crawling on her face.

Mrs. Alex stops talking fast, but only for a second.

"Let me tell you about the kids. She takes her papers out of her bag. I don't want to listen to her talk about our birth mother or how bad we are. She doesn't care that it hurts us. How would she like it if I told Jessica and Jason how bad she is as a person? I bet she wouldn't like it at all.

Jason's gaze moves to Curtis and me standing together in the doorway to the grape room. "Do you guys want to sit on the sofa?" He must've thought we didn't hear him, though he did get Mrs. Alex to shut up again for a second. I like that.

Sofa? What's a sofa? Great—here we go again with people using words I don't get. It took me forever to learn new words with the Stones, and now I hafta do it again. I don't move because I have no idea what a sofa is.

Mrs. Alex sits on the couch and pats the cushions next to her. "Come sit down, kids, while I give the Tubners information about you."

I don't move, and neither does Curtis.

Jason stands up. "I'll be right back." He disappears into another room.

Mrs. Alex begins her tale of Norma, my birth mother, just like she did at the old foster home and doesn't even care that we are standing right here. Our new foster mother keeps looking at us.

"Anna doesn't like to change her underwear, so you must watch in case she hides them."

Something punches me in the gut. Did this really happen? Did Mrs. Alex really tell this stranger about what I do with my underwear?

I can't get enough air into my lungs. I swear I would fall to the floor if Curtis wasn't holding onto me. It feels like an elephant is sitting on my chest. Nothing is working, no matter how hard I push at the big animal to get it off. It feels impossible to get air.

I try to take a deep breath but it's not working. All my body is doing is taking a lot of small fast breaths. I rub my hands together to get the sweat off.

"Mrs. Alexander, I'd prefer we finish our conversation about the children's mother another time." Jessica doesn't take her eyes off me, though she is talking to Mrs. Alex.

Everything in the room spins, but the pressure on my chest lightens a little.

"I don't have time later, so I need to give you the information."

"Here we go." Jason walks into the room carrying two big, blue, bean bag chairs like we had in my class at my last school. "How about these things? They are way more comfortable than an old sofa anyway." Jason steps in front of Mrs. Alex. "Sit on these, kids. I think you will like them." Jason nods and walks away.

I move to sit down on the bean bag chair because I'm afraid I will fall over. Curtis does the same and holds my hand as we sit next to each other in our chairs.

"Anna does—"

"Mrs. Alexander, I believe my wife asked you if we could have this conversation another time and not in front of the kids." He turns his head to look at us for a brief second before turning back to Mrs. Alex. "Now, please, respect our wishes. We can give you a call tomorrow or meet with you another time to finish this conversation." He walks to stand in front of Mrs. Alex who is still sitting on the couch.

I wouldn't argue with him if I was Mrs. Alex.

"Well, um, okay, I guess. But it's important to hear about Anna's struggles with school and her bad grad—"

"I don't believe we need to hear anything about school today since it's the end of May and first week of June and they don't start school 'til September. So, again…" Jason stands up, and so does his wife. He holds out his hand. "It's getting late and we can take it from here. But we'll be in touch." Jason kinda sounds like my old principal at my last school when he got mad at me for punching a girl who called my brother a mean name.

"Ah, okay." Mrs. Alex stands slowly. "Kids, be good for the Tubners. They are good people and will take care of you now." She taps my head and then Curtis's as she walks by us.

Then, she's gone like every other time we've seen her, leaving us with strangers in a house we don't know and telling us to be good.

The Tubners stand in front of Curtis and me as we watch her walk toward the door. She turns. "If you need anything give my office a call and I will do what I can to help." The door shuts and we are alone. Mrs. Alex is gone.

"That was awful," Jason whispers and grabs Jessica's hand. I hear him though, because he's standing in front of us.

"It sure was." Jessica kisses Jason's hand. "Let's help these poor babies." They smile at each other. I can't stop watching them. I've never seen big people so nice to each other. They act like teenagers in love. My last foster parents, Sue and Allen, were nice to each other, but they didn't kiss each other like these guys do.

Curtis squeezes my hand tighter. I stop looking at them and look at him for a second before looking back at our new foster parents.

Jason and Jessica look down at us as they stand in front of the chairs.

"Okay, are you two ready?" Jason asks.

Ready for what? I want to scream at both of them.

How can we be ready for something we have yet to learn about? We have no idea what to be ready for.

No idea.

So, *are* we ready? I don't know. I squeeze Curtis's hand tighter.

Chapter 3
Staircase Riding

Jason and Jessica stand next to each other, holding hands. Jessica glances up at Jason. "I have to get the animals into the barn for the night and turn the lights off. Can you take the kids up to their rooms and get them settled in?"

"Sure can."

She stands on her tiptoes to kiss Jason and then looks at us. "I'm glad you're here with us, kids, and I will talk more with you tomorrow. Good night kids." Her voice sounds like she has more air coming out than words. She smiles and waves at us as the door closes behind her.

"Well, let's get this show on the road," Jason says, singing. He stops quickly by the stairs and points to our garbage bags. "I thought I'd ask again. I can either take those bags to your rooms for you now, or you can empty them tomorrow by taking out the items and carrying them to your room yourself. Which do you prefer?"

This man uses fancy words. *Prefer* must mean what I want to do. "I'll take care of the bag tomorrow morning." I cross my arms and stomp my foot.

"Alrighty, then. Let me give you the tour. Up the stairs we go."

One. Two. Three. Four. Six. Ten. Thirteen. Seventeen. Twenty and twenty-one. Ah-phew. I am out of breath. No wonder he said the bags would hit all the steps. He was right about that.

We walk down the hallway, still holding onto the banister. "Anna, look over the railing," Curtis whispers from behind me.

"Whoa," Curtis and I say at the same time. I can look down to the first floor.

"I can't wait to ride this banister," I whisper to him.

"Yeah, me, too. But you can go first."

Of *course* my brother would say that; I always go first.

"It's high up, isn't it?" Jason's voice startles us, and Curtis jumps. 1

"Yeah, it is," I lean over the dark, brown railing gazing downward.

He corrects me. "You mean, *yes*, it is."

"Yeah, that's what I said."

"Miss Anna, the correct answer to that question is, "*Yes*, it is." I step back away from the rail and turn my head so Jason can see my face.

"Okay then." I smirk and put a hand on my hip, gripping my doll in the other. I tilt my head. "Yes. Yes. Yes, it is."

He chuckles. "Look at you, giving me sass. You must be a little spitfire. Okay, Miss Thing." Jason snaps his fingers in the air and moves his hand in a weird back and forth motion. He looks kinda weird, and I have no idea what it means, but I chuckle with him.

"Whatever you two do, please be careful." He leans over the railing next to us and puts his hand on the other side of it. "You see how far down that is?" I follow his eyes to the first floor. "You fall over this railing, and you won't be getting up. That's a long way down."

"You mean I can't jump over the railing and swing from that huge light right there?" I spot the ginormous, glass light with candles hanging in front of us. "I'm sure I can make it from here." I giggle. I like him 'cause he reminds me of my daddy and he's funny.

"Okay, jungle woman, let's not try that, okay?" Jason holds his hand up for a high-five.

I smack it. "Deal."

Curtis watches us as he stands next to me.

"Here we go. Room number one for Curtis."

Jason opens the door, and I see Curtis's bedroom before he does.

"Anna, step aside so your brother can see his room. Come out from behind your sister, Curtis. You're safe here."

Curtis walks slowly into his new bedroom.

Jason heads to the bed. "As you can see, I decorated this room like a sailboat." He walks to the dresser and picks up a small sailboat. "My most favorite boat of all time. I'll have to——" He turns to talk with Curtis while I stand in the doorway, but Curtis walks to his new bed.

My brother rubs the white bedspread that has a big blue anchor on it. "This is cool," Curtis says quietly.

"I'm glad you like it. Tomorrow, when you and your sister walk around the property to check things out, you'll see one of my old sailboats on the lake. Jessica put some pajamas in the dresser for you. Get them on, then meet me in the hallway."

"Okay." Curtis sounds better than he did earlier and he smiles at Jason. It's like his angry outburst in the car never happened.

"Your turn, young lady. Let's head to your room."

At the end of the hallway, Jason puts his hand on the door and turns to look at me while he opens it. "Last, but not least, you get the big room at the end."

The door creaks, but I don't think it means it's old. Everything in this house looks and smells brand new.

I step inside a princess castle. The bed has four poles that go to the ceiling with a pink sheet over the top of it. At both ends of the bed are pink curtains that tie to the big poles.

I stare.

"Do you like the canopy bed, Anna? Jessica decorated this room."

There's a princess lamp by the bed and a princess doll on the dresser. I don't want to hurt Jason's feelings, but this room is way too girly for me—well, except for the green walls. "Um... sure. It's pretty."

"Good. That will make Jessica happy. This is a girl's room so I'm not going to hang out in here. Go ahead and get your pajamas on. Jessica put some in there for you." He nods his head in the direction of a big

17

dresser with a gigantic mirror on top of it. "When you're done, come out and meet your brother and me in the hallway, and I'll show you your bathrooms."

"You'll show us to our bathrooms?"

"Yes, we all have our own bathrooms here. Your brother's is off of his bedroom, and yours is the next door down. Get dressed for the night, and I'll show you." With that, Jason turns and leaves my new room, closing the door behind him.

I sit on the giant princess bed for a second before I fall backward into the bedspread. It puffs up when I fall as if I'm falling into clouds. The blanket smells like sweet roses.

I close my eyes. *Jesus, it's me, Anna. I'm in a new foster home now with Jason and Jessica Tubners. They seem like friendly people so far, but, then again, I thought the same thing about Sue, and look what she did to me. I hope Jessica won't be like Sue. I hope she won't want girl time. My friend, Karen, said that mothers don't do that, so maybe it was just Sue and not me. I miss my friends, Jesus, and now I won't be able to see them anymore.*

Please send them a message for me. Tell them how happy they made me in school and tell them thank you *for sticking up for me against that mean girl, Alyssa, and... um...* A tear makes its way down my cheek. *Tell them I'll miss them. I better go. Jesus, because Jason is waiting for me in the hallway. I will talk with you soon. Love, Anna.*

"Look at your nightgown. It fits you perfectly, Miss Anna." Jason gives me a thumbs up like Fonzi on the television show. The longer I'm here, the more he reminds me of my daddy. My heart still hurts when I think and dream of Daddy. I wonder if it will ever feel better?

"Be careful going down the stairs with your gown down by your ankles. You might want to pick it up a little, so you don't trip." Jason cares if I trip down the stairs?

So far, he seems like a kind man. I hope it stays this way and he is not going to hurt me like Derek did in my first foster home. I hope he continues to act like my Daddy instead.

I hope.

Though my nightgown is plastered with pictures of princesses everywhere, it's super soft and silky.

"I like your cool pajamas, Curtis." His pjs have sailboats.

"Yeah, I guess." I can't see his mouth moving because he looks down. Even his shoulders look like they will drop off his body. He kinda looks like a sad donkey in one of the cartoons I watched at my last foster home with Sue.

"Let me show you your bathrooms." Jason walks down the hallway.

"On the right, we have the bathroom for Miss Anna Snow." Jason sounds like he has a microphone while he moves his hand up and down to show me the door. I chuckle. I can't help it because he is moving his legs up and down like he's a jack rabbit. Even Curtis looks up and giggles.

I walk into a bathroom with a double sink, and a pink shower curtain with a princess on it.

"In that drawer," Jason taps it with his finger, "you'll find a toothbrush. I'll leave you to it. Come, Curtis, your turn. I decorated your bathroom myself."

The door shuts, and they are gone. Jessica must have decorated this room, too, since it looks like princesses are everywhere. I'm sure Curtis's bathroom is going to be sailboats.

I have my own bathroom—something that's all mine.

I stand by the door, listening to Curtis and Jason talk as they walk back into Curtis's bedroom. Their voices fade until I can't hear them anymore. I lock the door, then move the handle to try to open it again just in case the lock doesn't work. I tug and tug, but the door won't budge.

Good.

Everything is pink in here, including my toothbrush. The shower curtain's pink and so is the curtain on the window, the towels, the rugs on the floor, and even the rug covering the toilet lid.

I've never seen a carpet on the toilet before, but I don't care. This is my *own* bathroom. No one can ever come in this room but me—and there's no Derek. It seems like a long time ago now, but I can still smell him and feel him hurting my girl parts. Instantly, I wrap my arms around the front of me because I feel cold and I'm shivering.

Anna, stop! He was in your first foster home. He can't hurt you here. Stop thinking about him.

That's right. Derek's not here. There's no way he can ever find me here, especially when *I* don't even know where I am.

Back in the hall, I stand next to Curtis as Jason claps his hands.

"Bedtime for you two. Tomorrow, we'll give you a tour of the house and the property. If you need anything, there are doorbells by each of your doors that will ring us in our bedroom downstairs. Good night and we'll see you in the morning."

Jason heads down the stairs while Curtis and I stare at each other.

"We have doorbells in our bedroom? Wow, fancy."

"I know," Curtis whispers.

"Jason seems nice." I bump Curtis with my hip.

"Yeah, I guess. But he's not Mom. I want to go home." A tear zigzags down his cheek, but he's not crying.

"Do you want to sleep in my room tonight with me? My giant bed is big enough."

At first, he says nothing. "Nah. I'm good." Without saying anything else, my brother goes into his room.

"Night, Curtis," I whisper. I wonder if he even heard me.

My brother is sad, and it's my fault, and there is nothing I can do to make it better. It's not like I can make us return to Sue and Allen's. I miss Sue, too, but I don't miss the girl time. And Curtis is right. She was a good mom to him because she didn't have secret girl time with him.

My ears get hot like a blow torch. Why did Sue have to ruin everything? Why couldn't she be a normal mom? I close my bedroom door behind me. The white wood going around my ceiling shines from the barn light coming through my bedroom window.

A noise comes from the barn. I kneel in front of my window and open it, looking for a ladder I can climb down.

Darn, there isn't one.

The noise sounds again. Two goats are walking around the pasture. One is all black, the other, white. They remind me of the goats at Mr. Bob's house at my first foster home. I can't wait to meet them. I like animals more than I like people. Animals have never hurt me before. I can't say the same about people.

"Hey goats, I'm Anna. I can't wait to meet you tomorrow. Maybe you'll become my new friends."

I really miss my animal friends. Especially Thunder. No other animal will ever be a better friend than he was. I made him feel happy when he was sad and hurt like me. And… he made me happy when I was sad and hurt. We were perfect for each other. He… was perfect. My nose twitches as my tears tickle it.

I bet he's neighing for me to come to visit him tonight.

I jump and run to bed, grabbing my Raggedy doll. Once again, she catches all my tears and makes them disappear into her skin. Thunder. I love and miss you. The tears pour out like a waterfall. I hiccup, and before long...

"Good morning!" Jason wakes me up the next morning by hollering up the stairs. "Rise and shine, it's time to feed yourself and the animals in the barn."

Animals! Great! I throw on the same clothes I'd worn yesterday because I still have to unpack our garbage bags today.

I knock on the door of Curtis's boat room.

He doesn't answer.

Hmmm.

I open the door.

His bed is made and all the lights are off.

I go to his bathroom. The door is open, but he's not in it—yup, I was right; it's all blue with white boat shapes everywhere.

I stop by his bed, turning to look around the room once more as if he would magically appear. Did he go downstairs without me? Does that mean he's mad at me? Does he know it's my fault we aren't at Sue and Allen's anymore?

I disappear into Curtis's blanket as I sit down on his bed. My heart hides itself because it knows all of this is its fault. If only—

"Anna, your brother is already down here. Come join us."

All I hear is Jason. I wonder if Jessica is in the house or out in the barn already. I hope not, because I want to go meet the animals with her. As I reach the top of the stairs, my hands freeze on the railing. This looks like it would be a fantastic ride.

Should I?

My hands then wrap around the dark brown railing sitting on top of a bunch of white spindles that follow the stairs down to the first floor. It's smooth and cool against my palm. Should I do it? I bet this would be super-fast.

It's as if my brain takes over and I can't control it, and down I go— faster than I'd anticipated. I slam into the wall, making a noise louder than thunder rumbling in the sky.

"Ouch!" My back hurts terribly, and before a tear can escape, Jason comes storming into the room.

"Anna, are you okay? What did you do, child?"

"I rode the railing." I keep my hand on my back, and I squeeze where it hurts. "My back hurts." If I say it any louder, I'll cry, because I feel like I am getting stitches again but this time all over my back. I don't want to do that in front of anyone, let alone someone I don't know because these new parents will think I'm a baby and not a big girl. I hafta show 'em how strong I am.

"Don't move, Anna. Jessica is a doctor, and she's coming." Jason sounds like he is far away. *She's a doctor? I live with a real life doctor?*

Within seconds, Jessica comes running through the front door. "What happened? Don't move her! "

Even when hollering, she still sounds like she's whispering.

"She slid down the railing," Jason says.

"Anna, don't move. I have to make sure you didn't break your back." I can't see her talking, but she sounds concerned, like the nurse in my old school did when I got sick. "I need to check you from your head to your feet for any bleeding. Then, I have to check your pelvic area that is located above your girl par—"

"No, don't! I didn't hurt my girl parts. Please don't." I stare at her in terror, and my heart races like a car engine. I don't want anyone to ever touch me again in my girl parts. I hurt my back so why does she have to check me there?

Just as I get ready to jump up and run away, she moves in front of my face so I can see her better. She leans down and whispers in my ear. "Anna, I am going to ask Jason to leave us alone. I won't hurt you. I'm not going to touch your girl parts. I'm going to touch this bone here." She points to her stomach. "Is that okay?"

Before I can answer, she looks at Jason. "Can you leave me with Anna for a few minutes? I'll call you if I need any help rolling her or if I need to get her on a stiff board. Wait on calling paramedics until I do my assessment."

"Call the paramedics? One is standing in front of you." Jason tilts his head to the side.

"Yes, I meant the ambulance. I'll call you if I need you."

"Anna, don't worry honey, you are in the best hands of any doctor around this area." With that, Jason leaves the room.

"Curtis, I see you in the doorway, and I am sure you're worried about your sister, but I've got this. Why don't you go with Jason into the family room?"

I can't see Curtis because my head is facing away from where he is.

"No, I won't leave my sister!" he yells.

"Anna, are you okay with Curtis staying here and watching us?"

"Yes." I cough. "Ouch that hurts." I cry out.

"I know it does, sweety, let's see what we have going on. Here we go. I'll tell you everything I'm doing. You will feel my hands, but don't move. Let me know if you feel any pain, though. The first thing I want you to try to do is wiggle your toes."

I move my toes.

"Good. Now, can you move your foot?"

I move my foot.

"Good. Now, can you move your leg a little and tell me if that hurts?"

I do so. "It's fine."

"Phew." Jessica lets out a massive breath like she's been holding it for hours. "Good. I'm relieved. Those are all great signs your back is okay. Let me check you for any bleeding or pain, and then we can roll you over. I'll let you know where my hands are going, okay?"

"Yeah."

"I have my hands on the back of your head and am going to check your neck. Just a little pressure. Can you feel my hands?"

"Yes."

"Does anything hurt?"

"No."

Jessica goes down my shoulders, my arms, my back, then around to my stomach. "Now, I'm going to check your pelvic bone, as I said before. Remember, I'm not going anywhere near your girl parts, I promise."

Jessica's hand moves around my back to my front, pushing on bones in my lower belly, nowhere near where I don't want her to be.

"Does this hurt?"

"No."

"Great. Can you feel my hands pushing on your pelvic bone?"

"Yes, I can."

"Fantastic. I think your back is okay."

Jessica removes her hand and moves to my legs and I feel every place she touches.

"Jason, can you come back in and help me roll her over? See, Curtis? Your sister is just fine. Well, maybe not fine, because she's going to be sore, but nothing appears to be broken. Kids, this is why we don't slide down that railing. It's way too steep, and, as you have seen, you'll fly into the door. So, no railing riding, you two. Got it?"

"Yes," we both answer at the same time. After this, I have no desire to ride that railing ever again, and it sounds like Curtis agrees with me. I mean, it was fun, but so not worth it.

Before long, I'm sitting up.

"Anna, let me look in your eyes." She shines a flashlight at me. "No sign of concussion." She puts the flashlight back in a black bag. "I want you to lie down and chill on the sofa for the next few hours." She turns around. "Jason, please take Curtis to the barn with you to finish the chores. I'll spend a little time with Anna to get to know her better."

"On it, baby. I'll give Curtis the tour and show him my sailboat and the lake, too." He smiles at Curtis.

"No. I want to stay with my sister." Curtis doesn't look at Jason, just me. "I want to make sure my sister's going to be okay." He looks up at Jason.

Jessica walks over and puts her hand on Curtis's shoulder. "No reason for you to be bored inside the house. I'll stay with her for the next few hours to make sure she's okay."

Jason clears his throat. "I hear you like fishing, Curtis. I have two poles in the barn. Are you up for it?"

"Yeah!" That's all it takes for my brother to smile, because he loves to fish, but it goes away as quickly as it came. He looks at me. "Um…"

"I'm okay. Go fish. I'll be fine." I say it to assure him, but am I really? What does alone time mean to Jessica? I found out what it meant to Sue, and I don't want to do that anymore. My stomach hurts.

"Okay." He nods at Jason, and they both leave the room.

"Let's get you up." Jessica reaches under my armpits. "Luckily, you're a tiny thing, so I don't need Jason's help and we can use some girl time anyway. The boys can do their own thing."

And there it is—*girl time*.

So, it *does* mean the same thing to Jessica that it meant to Sue.

No! No! I scream loudly in my head, but no one can hear it because the words won't come out of my mouth. My body floats across the floor under Jessica's arms. Why can't I tell her to stop it before she even tries? Why can't I just punch her so she won't make me do things I don't want to do to her? Why?

If I say anything, they will make us leave here too. I don't want to move again. I don't.

Curtis went fishing with Jason, who seems like a nice guy. Now, I'm going to ruin that, too, by telling Jessica *no*.

But I don't want to suck on her boobs like a baby.

My heart races, my head hurts, and my hands feel like sweat is dripping off them.

And I keep hearing the screams in my head.

But I can't ruin this for Curtis. I just can't. He finally seems happy. Oh… man.

Here we go, Anna…

Chapter 4
Sailboat

Jessica puts me down and her arm goes around my waist as we walk. "I'm glad the foyer is right off the living room. I don't want you walking too far. Let's go slowly, Anna. We're in no hurry to get where we're going."

She *sounds* nice… but so did Sue.

I really don't want to do this.

We're back to the couch. "Sit down. I'll be right back."

She opens the cabinet and pulls out a blanket.

Great. She's gonna cover me up so no one can catch us when they come in. At least Sue had me go to her bedroom.

I don't want Jason or Curtis to see, but I can't do anything to mess this up. I can't make Curtis move again.

"Here we go. A blanket for us during girl time." Jessica sits next to me, then turns on the television.

A lady on the screen runs out of her seat, screaming as she jumps up and down in front of a dollar sign.

"This is my favorite television show. I like to try and guess the price of things." Jessica claps her hands together. Her dimples pop and I can see all of her straight, white teeth that look nothing like my buck teeth. I jump as she touches my leg with her hand. It feels like she stabbed me and my heart races. "Let's get you covered up. Jason likes to keep the air-conditioner on so high, it freezes us all out."

The soft blanket feels good. That is… until Jessica rests her hand on my leg. Though she does it on top of the blanket, it feels like her touch is burning a shape into my skin.

My stomach twists and, all of a sudden, I feel like I'm going to be sick.

I wrap my arms around me, trying to stop the puke. I know what alone time with a foster mother means. Jessica calls this girl time, so I know what she wants me to do. Thinking about girl time makes my stomach hurt badly.

She stands and walks out of the room without saying a word. Is she mad at me because I didn't move towards her boobies? Why did she leave and not say anything to me? Though I feel some relief, my stomach continues to clench. I try to slow my breathing and focus on the TV show. If I think about something else other than feeling sick, maybe I won't throw up.

She comes back into the room a few minutes later with two big, brown cups in her hands. "Here we go. Hot chocolate for girl time. One for you and one for me." She seems so cheerful and acts happy that we're here, or is she just happy because she's going to make me touch her boobies? Is this why foster mothers want foster daughters?

"One-thousand, five hundred, and fifty-five dollars." Jessica stays seated but bounces around on the sofa and yells at the television. "Anna, you have to bid on all the items on stage. So, we have to guess the price for the washing machine, dryer, and a weekend getaway to the Poconos."

She sips her hot chocolate. "Mmmm. Yummy." Her eyes don't move from the television. I wish she would get it over with and not

27

pretend she's excited to watch this show. My last foster mother would pretend to do something I liked, but it was only to get me to her bedroom to suck her boobies. Now Jessica is pretending to be happy about watching this stupid television show and drinking hot chocolate with me, when all she cares about is making me do things to her that I don't wanna do.

I cross my arms and get angrier with each passing moment. She's faking it all. I know what she wants me to do, so why is she taking so long to make me do it? Let's just get it done already. I squeeze both of my upper arms tighter. If only Thunder was outside in her barn. I would jump on his back and run away.

For a second, all of me is crying. Every muscle in my body hurts. Every bone... feels broken.

I am... broken.

I want Thunder and I want my daddy back. They would protect me from this new foster mother and take me away from this.

The man on the TV yells into his microphone, "One thousand, four hundred, and seventy-five dollars."

"I knew it!" Jessica clicks her cup against mine. "Isn't girl time fun?" She stares at me.

"Um... yeah. I guess..."

Jessica beams with joy. I squeeze my arms tighter. My lungs feel like they are full and I'm having a hard time getting air. I breathe faster. She turns her head and glances at my face, and then turns her eyes to my stomach.

"Am I making you uncomfortable sitting next to you, Anna? I thought you might like some company while you chill out. I don't like to be alone when I get hurt, plus, I want to be able to keep an eye on you." Jessica then pulls the little flashlight out of her pants pocket. "Let's see how those pupils are doing."

The light hurts my eyes for a second but then she's done. "Your eyes look great, and there's no dilation of the pupils. This is good. You'll be up in no time."

The front door opens with a loud *bang* as it hits the wall.

"Easy, Bub. We don't want to leave marks on the wall." Jason puts a hand on the door and it stops moving. "You guys should have seen how many fish Curtis caught. It's like he called them to him or something." Jason gives him a thumbs-up.

"I beat him." He holds his finger over his shoulder, pointing behind his back at Jason. "I caught four fish, and Jason didn't catch any."

Jason smacks Curtis on the back. "Head upstairs and change your clothes so you don't smell like fish. Then we can get ready for a late lunch."

Curtis heads up the fancy staircase to his room without a word.

"How's she doing, honey?" Jason comes over and kisses Jessica's lips *right* in front of me.

"Ewww," I say out loud.

Jason burst into laughter.

"She's good. No evidence of a concussion so far. We enjoyed our girl time. She watched me bid on things I can't win through the television set."

"Sorry, Anna, that Jessica made you sit through that boring show for your time together." Jason winks then walks into another room.

Jessica squints her eyes together and moves her head closer to me. "I think you're good to get up and move around. Thank you for our girl time and the hot chocolate toast."

This is her idea of girl time? She didn't ask me to do anything to her boobs. She didn't ask me to cuddle with her. She didn't ask anything. Nothing.

I stare at Jessica's back as she leaves the room and goes in the same direction that Jason did.

Curtis's feet pound the wooden steps to go upstairs to his bedroom.

I stand and test my balance. All good. I walk to the staircase carefully because my back is sore, just like they said it would be. My brother waits patiently, halfway to the top, for me before he takes another step.

"You seem better, Curtis. Are you feeling happier?"

He locks eyes with me, but I see nothing. His eyes look as flat as the stones he likes to throw in the water. "I'm... um... fine."

"Did you like fishing with Jason?"

Curtis heads up the stairs again without answering. After a few more steps, he stops to look at me. "I guess." He turns away and climbs the rest of the stairs.

I walk back to the sofa. I watch people trying to win money on the television while my new foster parents laugh with each other in the kitchen. I wish I could be happy like that—but how can I be when no one wants us?

Curtis comes flying down the stairs, runs into the living room, and

29

then plops himself next to me. He doesn't say anything. So I don't either. A wave of sadness hits me. My brother doesn't love me anymore.

During a laundry detergent commercial, Curtis clears his throat. "I miss Mom and I want to go back home. I will never have another mom ever again. I never want a mom ag—"

"Who's ready to grab something to eat? I don't know about you two, but it's been a long morning, and I'm hungry." Jason walks back into the room and waves his arm for us to follow him. Any mention of food and Curtis will follow anyone.

"Whoa," Curtis says rather loudly.

We go into the kitchen. "Holy crap." The ceiling is taller than a tree. It's even higher than my old church, and it has giant fans hanging down.

"You two are going to break your necks." Jason tickles under my chin. I giggle.

"How tall is that ceiling?" I point.

His head goes back as he looks up. "Good question. I have no idea."

"I thought the kitchen at my old house was big, but this place is ginormous."

"Yes, it is. Jessica works hard for us to have nice things." He hugs her from behind while she cooks. These two are always hugging or kissing. It's so gross. I've never seen big people act so lovey-dovey before. It makes me feel weird. I look away.

Curtis is already sitting at the table eating a grilled cheese sandwich. "Yum, Anna, wait 'til you taste this. So, so good." He hums in enjoyment as he chews.

This may be okay. Maybe he won't be so mad anymore and will like Jessica and Jason. Even more—maybe he will love me again.

"Do you two want to go to the barn later when we do barn chores?"

Curtis is fast to answer. "Yes, I do!"

"Me, too. Definitely." Inside I'm smiling. My back hurts a little from my ride on the railing, but I ignore it. No way am I sitting on that couch all day.

"I think you'll like the animals," Jessica sits a cup of orange juice in front of me.

"I love animals, Jessica. Do you have a horse? I really miss my last horse called Thunder." I hold my breath. It would make this place even more groovy.

A chair scrapes across the white, tiled floor in the kitchen as Jessica sits next to me. "Honey, I know how much you miss Thunder. I miss my animals too when they are no longer with me or when they go to heaven. We once had a big Irish Wolfhound Dog named Dughal. He got sick and passed away. It's been a year since he's been gone and… I still think about him all the time." Jessica's head falls to her chest, and she sniffles.

She looks up and I feel the weight of her hand on my leg. I look down. It feels like I got a giant needle in the exact spot she's touching. My heart beats faster. I move my leg. I don't like anyone touching me. It really feels like their skin is burning me. It hurts.

She jerks her hand back. "I'm sorry. I didn't mean to make you uncomfortable."

I keep looking at my grilled cheese sandwich while saying nothing.

"Unfortunately, we don't have a horse. And, I don't think getting one is a good idea either because Jason and I have no clue how to care for such a big animal. I'm sorry, hon—"

"Who needs a horse when you have Twinkles and Sticks?" Jason says from across the kitchen. "Wait 'til you meet them. They'll love you too. So will the kittens and the barn ca—"

"Cats and kittens? My chair hits the floor as I jump out of it. "You have cats and kittens?" I run to Jason in the archway, not caring about my juice or grilled cheese.

"How about we eat lunch first? Then you can go to the barn with Jason."

I turn toward Jessica's voice as she picks up the chair I knocked over. "I'm not hungry. I want to see the kittens and the cats. I want to go outside now. *Please*."

Jason helps Jessica with the chair. "Anna, Jessica asked you to eat the lunch she prepared first and since she never cooks," he winks at Jessica, "we should show her how much we appreciate it by eating it."

I haven't been here long, but I can tell that Jason always sticks up for Jessica, so, I guess I better do what she asks me from now on.

My shoulders drop as I walk back to my chair. "Fine." I sit and eat my sandwich as fast as I can—and agree with Curtis; this sandwich is fantastic. "Yum, this is good."

We're finally outside, and I can't get to the barn fast enough.

"Anna, hurry up! I want to show you the goats!" Curtis yells as he runs ahead of me to the barn.

I sprint to catch up. I can't wait to see the goats. But I don't have far to run because, all of a sudden, two goats run out of the barn at full speed right at me.

I freeze because, at Daddy's house, Mr. Bob's goats liked to jump on me, and running away from them only made them jump on my back. So, I stand still.

Within seconds, the two of them are rubbing up against my legs like cats do.

"Hey, Sticks. Hey, Twinkles."

"Jason, why do they sound like crying babies?"

Jason laughs as he dumps the grain into their dish. "Good question. I don't know how to answer that. But I agree with you, they sound like they're saying *mom* like a child would do."

He's right. The more I listen, the more I hear it. Mom. Mom. Mom. It really sounds like they are saying mom. I giggle.

"Sticks, get down," I scream as she jumps up on me. I dart away.

Curtis is on the barn floor with Twinkles all over him and he's giggling.

I like seeing that so much. My heart hurts when I see he's sad. It makes me wanna cry. I'd rather laugh with him.

Twinkles keeps walking around Curtis and won't let him up..

Meoow. Meoow.

I turn. I can't believe what I am seeing. At first, my feet wouldn't move for me. Can it be? Can it be? There in front of me is a black kitten with green eyes.

"Lucky!" I run to the kitten.

"It looks like you've met Midnight." Jason's voice snaps me out of my head. "Who's Lucky, Anna?"

"Lucky's her old kitten at our last-last house," Curtis blurts out to Jason.

Every new home reminds me of something from my old ones. These goats remind me of Mr. Bob's goats. Midnight looks exactly like Lucky, my old kitty I brought back to life after my brother tried to drown her in the creek.

There are five more kitties here—a white one with a black tail, an orange one, two black-and-white ones, one all-black one, and one gray. I sit on the ground, and they climb over me, acting like I'm their mama. My heart feels like singing.

32

"Look at that, Anna. The kitties love you."

"I love them."

"All of them, except the black one, will be leaving later today to go to a new home. They are old enough to leave now." Jason glances at Lucky—I mean, Midnight.

"Can I keep her? Can I please if no one is picking her up? Can I call her Lucky, too?"

Jason puts the pitchfork down and looks at me for a second. "I don't see why not—as long as you promise to feed her and take care of her. And she also has to stay in the barn. Okay?"

I jump up and down like I'm jumping rope with Lucky in my arms. "Thank you! I will take care of her. Thank you, Jason." I kiss the kitty's head. "Lucky is your new name. I hope you like it." I grab my back, it hurt a little with all my jumping around.

"You sure you're feeling okay, Anna?"

"I'm okay." I don't want to tell him I'm a little sore, but I'm not really lying. I hit the wall pretty hard, but it's no big deal. I've hurt way worse in my first foster home when my foster brothers made us play the book game and shot at us with a BB gun. My back hurting is nothing compared to that.

"Follow me, and I'll show you the backyard with the lake and go over all the rules about the water." Jason walks past the kittens and me.

"Come on, Anna, you *got* to see this *huge* pond. We can skip rocks forever." Curtis jumps up and runs outside the barn.

"Let's go, Lucky." I pick up my new kitty and tuck her into my shirt. As I leave the barn and lay my eyes on the water, I think better of it. I put the kitten down and promise Lucky, I'll return soon.

A rock dances across the water before Jason and I reach Curtis.

"Wow, did you make this pond, Jason?"

"No. We built the house next to the lake."

"What's a lake? Isn't it a pond?"

Jason chuckles a little.

"A pond is much smaller than a lake, and you are right. Ponds, many times, are man-made, but a lake is not, per se."

Whatever, per se, means, but I don't really care because I want to throw rocks. As my first stone hits the water, I see it.

A boat flies by us, towing a person on two pieces of wood, and water goes everywhere. That looks like so much fun. "What are they doing?" I ask Jason, who's picking up rocks from the little sand beach and putting them by the big wooden walkway that goes out into the water. "Can I do that?" I cross my fingers.

"Sorry, Anna, I only have a sailboat, and that doesn't have a motor to pull you behind it for waterskiing. Plus, that lake is bottomless, and I know one hundred percent that Jessica will not let either of you on any boat until you take swim lessons."

Great, another foster mother who's going to stop me from doing what I want. My first foster mother, who made me call her Mother, was mean and didn't like me, but maybe, that wasn't so bad because I got to do what I wanted to do all day when she locked me out of her house. She only let me in the house to eat lunch. My newer foster mothers, like Sue and Jessica, are way more protective and don't let me do whatever I want. If Jessica wouldn't care what I'm doing, like Mother didn't, I could wave my hands to get the boat people to come over so I can jump on those ski things.

Jason taps my shoulder and interrupts the plans I'm making. "Come here. Let me show you my sailboat."

We walk over to a broken-down shed on the water. "Where's the ground?"

"There's no floor. This is a lake shed that I store my boat in." He bends down and kicks the top of the water with his foot. The boat is huge. It's white and spotless. On the side, it reads, *Jessica.* He named his boat after her? He must really love her like Daddy… loved me. I bet if my first daddy had a boat, he would have named it after me.

"There isn't enough wind today to take her out. The wind makes her move." Jason uses big words to talk about the sail and how it has to move to make the boat go, but my eyes stay glued to the person water skiing.

I want to do that because it looks like fun, and I love the water. "Jason?"

He stops fixing the rope on his boat and looks up.

"When are swim lessons?"

"There's another round of them in late July. Jessica is a swim instructor. I'll tell her to get you signed up if you want to learn."

"What is a swim instructor?" He has to stop using big words that I don't understand.

Jason grunts as he lifts the boat further out of the water with ropes. "She teaches people how to swim."

"Wow, she does everything. She's a doctor and teaches people to swim. She's super groovy." For the first time, I feel happy about being in a new place. Maybe this place is going to be a lot of fun. Jumping up and down, I clap my hands. "Curtis, do you want to do them with me? Do ya?"

A rock jumps in and out of the water like it's dancing to the music coming from the boat that speeds by us once more.

"Nope. I don't." My brother is back to not saying much.

"Come on, do it with me. It will be so much fun." I bump his shoulder, and the rock he's about to throw flies toward the direction of the old barn holding the sailboat.

Jason jumps. His boat is halfway in the old barn and halfway out. Curtis missed hitting the boat by inches.

"Please tell me that wasn't a rock." For the first time, Jason sounds kinda mad.

Curtis puts his head down.

"Sorry, Jason, it was my fault. I bumped my brother's arm as he was throwing the rock."

"Be careful. I don't want any rocks near this boat. Okay?"

"Yup, got it!" I holler back.

"Curtis, did you hear me?"

My brother doesn't look up at him and, instead, stares at the heart-shaped, gray rock in his hand. "Yup," he hollers over the crashing waves as another boat approaches.

Jason goes back to winding up his rope after Curtis answers him. I pick up a rock and stand next to my brother and then lift my arm to throw it.

"Leave me alone." Curtis's face is red. "You got me in trouble. Get away from me."

"No, I didn't, and I'll throw the rock if I wanna." What I want to do is cry and punch my brother at the same time. I'm mad. Why is he trying to hurt me? I didn't get him into trouble. Why is he blaming me? I pick up another rock.

Curtis hollers louder than I've ever heard him, louder than he was in the car yesterday. "Get away from me." He pushes me, knocking us both over into the sand.

I jump up, and so does my brother. I grab him by the shoulders and then shove him to the ground again. Before long, we're rolling around and hitting each other. The gritty sand wraps around my body as we roll.

Chapter 5
Garbage Bag Life

"Ouch! Let go of my hair!" I holler as loud as I can at my brother, who's pulling on my hair so hard, I swear he's going to rip it out of my head. "Curtis, stop it!" The pain rips through me. I can't help but cry out as Curtis is lifted in the air.

"That's enough of that." Jason's voice thunders in my ears.

I look up as Jason lifts Curtis up by his shorts and then lays him on the sand. "Can someone please tell me what is going on here?"

"An… na hit me fir… st," Curtis thrashes around to get away from Jason.

"No, I didn't. You hit me first!" I growl at him.

Curtis swings at me and misses my face by an inch. I scramble up

36

and jump toward him as he escapes from Jason's grip. Before long, we're back to rolling around.

"I hate you. I hate you!" Curtis sounds like a wounded animal as he hisses at me.

Once again, he is lifted off me.

"Curtis, that's enough! Now get yourself into the house, young man."

My brother jerks out of Jason's grip. "Fine." He spits at me.

"Curtis, go now." Jason points at the house.

I stand with Jason and fight the flood of tears that want to fall out of me, ready to join the water in the lake. I breathe fast, trying to get air. It's not working. I feel like an elephant is sitting on my chest.

Jason steps in front of me and puts his hands on my shoulders. "What happened?"

My throat feels thick and I shake all over with sadness and anger at the same time. "I don't... know." I study the sand stuck to my shoes.

"That didn't look like an 'I don't know' to me. Let's head inside so we can have a conversation with your brother." Jason's hand, on my shoulder, guides me in the direction of the house.

"What the heck happened?" Jessica meets us at the door. "Curtis came storming into the house and ran upstairs."

"Jessica, why don't you take Anna into the kitchen while I follow up with Curtis." Jason slides his hand up the railing as he runs, acting like it's a cane holding him up.

Once in the kitchen, Jessica wastes no time. "Tell me what happened outside."

I repeat the same thing I told Jason. What more can I tell her that I didn't tell him already?

I put my head down. I don't want to answer Jessica's questions right now. I don't want them to be mad at Curtis. But... she is standing in front of me with her face almost touching mine and I don't think I have an option to ignore her right now. She's not moving and I can feel her breath on my cheek.

"My brother's mad. That is all I know."

"Anna, look at me please?"

Slowly, I raise my head and see her big, sad eyes. "Are you sure you don't know why?" She motions for me to sit in a chair at the table next to her.

"I don't know what the hell is my brother's problem!" I scream at her as loud as I can and throw the chair across the room. It smashes through the sliding glass door. My heart breaks like the glass shattering everywhere. Why did my brother hurt me? Why is he so mad at me? My brother hates me.

"Anna."

Jessica's whisper brings me out of my mind. "Your brother and Jason are coming down. Let's see what we can discover, because we cannot have you fighting each other." Jessica's usual smile now is a straight line. She reaches over to move my hair out of my eyes and tucks it behind my ears. "I'm just trying to help and I'm worried about you."

Curtis pulls a chair away from the table, but yanks it back so hard it hits the table leg.

Jason sits next to him. "Please be careful. We don't want marks all over our furniture." He acts friendly, but I know they're mad at us right now because we have to sit at this table and talk to them.

"Why are you so mad at your sister?" Jason leans closer to Curtis.

My brother says nothing.

"Curtis, please talk with us. We can help you and your sister." Jessica tries to get him to talk.

He puts his head on the table.

"Anna, do you want to tell us what happened?"

Why do they think I have a clue what made Curtis so mad? I'm shocked by him, too. How can I answer them when I don't know?

Then, without another word, Curtis gets up and runs back upstairs.

The grown-ups let him go.

"Anna, why don't you go back outside for a little while? Give Curtis space, and after he calms down, maybe we can try to talk it out again." Jason puts his hand on Jessica's shoulder as he talks to me. These two people have no clue who my brother is. He won't calm down anytime soon.

I walk toward the front door, but I stop when I see our garbage bags. "Do you want me to take care of our stuff?" I open my bag as Jason comes into the foyer.

"Nope, not now. Go outside and get some space from each other, and we can take care of that later."

"Okay." He doesn't have to tell me that twice because I'd rather be in the barn with the animals who love me, than in the house with a brother who's mad at me.

38

Just as the door closes, the waterfall happens. Within seconds, I'm tasting the tears that find their way to my mouth and wiping away the snot that escapes my nose. My brother must know I told on our old mother, saying that I didn't want secret girl time. He must understand that it's my fault we had to leave. That's why he's so mad.

I head to Sticks' and Twinkle's pen, then sit in the hay. The straw stabs my skin as I curl up into a ball in the middle of the stack, but I don't care how much it hurts, because nothing is as bad as I feel right now.

My brother hates me. He... hates me.

Tears fall as my body shakes all over—even my feet are moving. It's like my body is pushing all of the sadness out through my tears that I keep trapped so no one can see me cry like a baby. But—I can't help it right now. I can't hold them in any longer. My brother is all I have in this world. I have no one else. I don't have a mom. I don't have a dad. I just have Curtis.

For the first time since I left Daddy, I cry as if I broke my leg. Why does this happen to me? Why does my life have to be so hard? Why doesn't anyone want Curtis and me? I hate my life and don't want to live it anymore.

My loud crying draws the attention of the barn animals. Sticks curls up next to me and I wrap my arm around her, so she doesn't run away. Lucky joins us, snuggling up to us.

"Thank you, Lucky. How did you know I needed a hug?" Her fur tickles my nose as I kiss the top of her head. "Thanks, Sticks, you didn't leave either or hurt Lucky. I'm proud of you." I rub Stick's fur.

Lucky doesn't move. Instead, she curls up in a ball in the hay with me.

"Jesus, are you there? I really need your help right now. I know you probably think that I always ask you for help. But I really need it now. My brother hates me, and he pushed me down and pulled my hair. Why would he do that? Is the devil making him do that? Please help him. I don't want him to be mad at me. I love him, and only me and Curtis are in this world you made. Why would you want him and me to be alone without any big person to take care of us? Why would you do that to us?" I cry harder. *"Why Jesus? Why?"* I lie still, holding Lucky, and waiting to hear Jesus's voice. I need him to talk to me so I don't feel alone.

But the only voice I hear is Twinkles', who stands in front of us, making noises that sound like *mom.* Sticks never leaves my side.

Twinkles stops talking, which is good because I need it to be quiet to hear Jesus.

"Anna." Someone is pushing my arm.

I open my eyes and Jason's face is the first thing that comes into focus.

"What are you doing sleeping out here? You could have come into the house to take a nap."

"Huh?" I rub my eyes and yawn.

Lucky climbs out of my shirt, and Twinkles jumps up and catches my arm with her sharp hoof.

"Come on, Anna, help me feed these goats since they like you so much." Jason holds out his hand for me to grab. He lifts me to my feet while I hold onto Lucky with my other arm.

The hay crunches under my feet as I follow Jason to the grain bin. "One pound of grain per goat each day." The grain makes a lot of tingling noises as it falls into the dish. "Now, let's also make sure they always have some alfalfa." It feels prickly in my hand as I drop the wad Jason had me carry to the cage.

"Here you go, Twinkles and Sticks." If my brother doesn't love me anymore, maybe these new barn friends will.

"Let's head back in the house so you can unpack your bags." Jason winks and smiles so big his eyes get squinty.

I bet he wouldn't be so happy if his whole life was in bags, like mine and Curtis' are. He wouldn't be so happy if he was garbage like us.

Once we're in the house, Jason grabs my bag right away.

"I think I know the answer, but it won't hurt to ask again." Jason stands, holding only my stuff.

My head tilts to the side. "Where is the other one?"

"When you were napping in the barn earlier, your brother took his bag up to his bedroom and put his stuff away." Jason walks toward the stairs.

This *is* a big deal. My brother doesn't take care of the stuff in his garbage bag, let alone carry it. I do that.

"He did what?" I snarl like a mad dog.

Now Jason is the one tilting his head and trying to raise his eyebrows to meet his hairline. "Is there a problem with that?"

Should I tell Jason everything I'm thinking? Would he even understand how I feel? How could he? I bet no one ever gave him away. He might think it's just a stupid garbage bag.

Jason's voice brings my attention back to him as he's standing in front of the staircase. "Do you want me to carry this garbage to your room so it is easier for you to take care of?"

Garbage? I guess he got that right.

"I'm sorry, Anna. I meant garbage *bag*. Why don't you let me carry this to your room so it'll be easier for you?" Jason puts his foot on the first step of the staircase.

I yank the bag out of his hand—and it slips out of my hand, slamming to the floor. "No! I can do it myself." I grip the black, plastic with both hands.

"Okay, okay, Spitfire, it's all you. But don't carry the bag upstairs because I don't want it scraping up the steps. So, please take items out of it and carry them upstairs. Okay?" Jason stares at me, his dark brown eyes like mine.

"Okay. I will."

Jason leaves me to my garbage.

***

Humpf. I make my last trip up the super steep staircase with my belongings. My legs burn with each step. The bag makes crinkle noises as I hold it up, making sure not to hit the steps. Jessica finally let me carry it upstairs because it's almost empty.

My legs feel like gelatin so I grab the railing at the top of the stairs, hoping it holds me up. I look over and see the round carpet in the foyer on the white tile floor with blue flowers swirling all over it. This house is like a pretty flower—so girly and beautiful.

"Anna? Is that you?"

The sound of my brother's voice stabs me in the heart as it echoes from his room and down the hallway because it's the first time he's spoken to me since our fight. A tornado of feeling sad and happy hit me at once. I turn to face my brother's door.

I freeze, hoping my mind isn't making up things right now that I wish I could do or hear.

It happens again.

"Anna?" His voice pulls my heart to follow it no matter how mad I am.

41

Chapter 6
Glass Bird

I grab my garbage bag and walk toward Curtis' room. I set it down before I push his door open, which squeaks like a tiny mouse.

As soon as I see his face, I can tell he's been crying.

"I'm sorry, Anna. Please don't hate me."

Curtis slams into me, almost pushing me to the ground.

"I don't know why I'm so mad, but I don't want to be here. I want to go home. I want to go back to Mom. I don't want to live in this house with these people."

I can't help it. I hug my brother. My tears fall onto his head, but I'm sure his hair stops him from feeling their wetness. I whisper so no one else can interrupt us. "I'm sorry, too. I wish we could go back there."

No matter how much I hate secret girl time, seeing my brother hurting this much is way worse. "Do you want to go outside and throw rocks?" That'll get his attention.

He steps back. "*Do* I? Let's go!" With that, Curtis runs downstairs, racing me to see who's the fastest—just like old times, two foster homes ago. We'd race each other to see who could get to the creek first. Though he is smaller than me, and younger, sometimes he'd beat me.

The front door slams behind him before I can even put my garbage bag in my bedroom. By the time I reach the top of the steps, Jason and Jessica are both standing in the foyer, watching me sprint down the stairs as fast as I can.

"Be careful! Don't fall down those stairs!" Jason warns.

. "Are you two okay now?"

I stop at the bottom. "Yeah, we are. We're going to throw rocks, his favorite thing to do," I reply in a soft voice while walking by them to the door.

"We really should talk about what happened," Jessica says as she puts her hand on my back. "Anna, it's not okay for your brother to hurt you like that. We need to talk about it."

No way is that gonna happen. It will only make Curtis mad to bring it up now. He's better, so I want them to leave him alone. "That's okay, we don't need to talk about it."

They stare at me like I have two heads.

"Okay honey, if that's what you think, but we like to resolve things in this family and talk about how we feel, especially when one person is mad. But if you want to leave it alone, we can respect your decision for now—as long as there aren't any more fights."

Jessica smiles as I shut the door behind me, then I run as fast as I can to catch up with Curtis, who's already standing by the lake and throwing one of who-knows-how-many rocks, and singing as he counts the number of times it skips across the water.

"Woohoo! I did it, Anna! Did you see that I made that rock skip seven times? I am the best rock-skipper ever." He jumps up and down like he's on a trampoline.

"Curtis, you're a really good rock-skipper, just like you're a good fisherman." I like to remind my brother how good he is at things.

Before too long, Jason yells that it's time to eat.

Curtis turns his head toward Jason's voice and instantly his face turns bright red and the vein in his neck pops out.

"I don't want to go into that house, Anna. I want to go home, and I want to go back to my mom and go back to my old room. I want to go back to my army men."

The lake water feels cold when it hits my feet as I step closer to my brother. "Didn't you bring your army men with you? Did you unpack them yet? Jason said that you took your bag upstairs earlier today."

Curtis' head snaps in my direction. His eyes lock on me like magnets on a refrigerator. He wrinkles his lips together and squints his eyes. "No, I didn't find my army men yet because I didn't put the stuff in my bag away. Jason asked if he could carry the bag upstairs and I told him yes, but I didn't take care of anything yet. I don't want to. I don't want to unpack it. I want to take that bag and run out of this house and run back to Mom, Anna. I want to run back to Mom!"

I grab my brother's hand.

He doesn't pull away as he throws another rock.

My whispers join the music of the crashing lake wave. "I wish we could do that, too, but we can't, Curtis." I put my head down and fight back the tears. My heart is being ripped apart like paper. I hate seeing my brother sad. There is nothing I can do to help him. Nothing.

I sniffle and wiggle my nose, hoping this stops my tears from flooding my eyes.

I can't help him.

If I could go back to Sue, even if she made me do girl time, I'd do it. Seeing my brother hurting and sad is way worse than girl time.

My stomach moves fast, like it always does when I'm upset, and I breathe faster and faster. "I wish we could go back, too. I really wish we could, Curtis."

My brother pulls his hand from mine and throws another rock.

"Hey, you two, it's time to get in the house to eat dinner. I called for you a little bit ago. Didn't you hear me? Come on, let's get going. Jessica made a good dinner and she's waiting on us." Jason is coming across the yard in our direction.

Maybe we can act like we didn't hear him the first time so we don't get in trouble.

I grab Curtis's hand again. "I know you don't want to be here, but they do seem like good people. Don't you think so?"

My brother shrugs. "I guess so."

I squeeze his hand. "So far, they have not been mean or even acted mad."

For the first time in a long time, Curtis turns his head and looks at me and then to Jason. "Yeah, you may be right. They do seem like nice people and Jason seems like a cool guy." Curtis looks at the boat parked in the water barn by the lake. "I also think that I could catch really big fish on that boat, so maybe I'll ask him to take me out fishing."

I laugh with my brother as he lets go of my hand to throw the last rock into the lake before walking toward Jason.

Though he's trying to act like he's happy, I know his heart is hurting—just like mine is for him. There's nothing I can do to help my brother.

Jason's voice makes its way across the yard. "You two are in for a treat tonight. Wait 'til you taste Jessica's lasagna."

Curtis stops walking instantly and can no longer hold back his tears. Without warning, he turns around and runs toward the boat shed.

My feet can't move as if they are stuck in quicksand and my brain isn't working. I don't know what to do. I don't know what to say. All of the air in my lungs escapes out through my mouth. I take a deep breath hoping it helps to stop my eyes from flooding with water. As I look up, a gust of wind slaps my face as Jason sprints by me, like he's running a race.

"Anna, please go into the house and help Jessica set the table for dinner. I need to check on your brother. I'll bring him in, sweetheart, so head in…"

Jason's too far away for me to hear the rest of what he's saying.

But I'm not going anywhere. I can't. I can't move. I don't *want* to move. I hafta see if my brother is okay, but I don't want to ignore what Jason asked me to do.

The bottom line, my brother is more important than setting the table.

I ignore his request and walk quietly to where Jason and Curtis are standing together, leaning against the side of the barn.

"Hey, buddy. What did I say that upset you?"

Curtis doesn't answer. Jason's eyes are so focused on my brother. I wonder if he sees that I'm standing at the edge of the barn behind him. I don't think Curtis sees me because he's too busy looking down at his feet.

"Curtis, buddy, I can help you, but I need you to tell me what it is that I said that upset you. You were smiling until I mentioned to you what Jessica was cooking for dinner. What upset you?" Jason moves from foot to foot like he can't stand on both of them at the same time.

My brother lifts his head. "Lasagna. That's what you said that upset me," he mumbles while still looking down.

Jason repeats what Curtis said. "Help me understand. Why does that upset you?" Jason leans into Curtis as if he thinks my brother will whisper his darkest secret—but he clearly doesn't know my brother because Curtis will nev—

"Mom… our last mom would make lasagna for us all the time. It was my favorite meal that she made for me. I want to go home, Jason. I want to go back to my mom." Curtis begins to cry again. For a minute, Jason stands like a statue, staring at Curtis. He has his hand on my brother's back.

I can't believe he told Jason why he's upset. I've never heard him talk to someone like that… besides me. Most of the time, he won't tell *me* what's bothering him either.

"How about this?" Jason's mouth is closer to my brother's ear now. "We have some good cereal in the house. Would you like to have that, instead, tonight with me? I think that's actually a great idea, because I don't have time to have cereal before I have to leave for the barn in the morning. So, you just gave me a good excuse to let Jessica know that I would rather have a big ol' bowl of cereal tonight for dinner rather than her cooking."

My brother raises his head and looks at Jason.

"How about it, buddy?" Jason grins.

I can't believe Jason can't see me standing right next to him. But, then again, he's too focused on my brother to notice me.

Curtis nods. "I like cereal. That would be better than lasagna. Thanks, Jason."

"All right then, let's get going. I think your sister is already in the house. How about we get a move on?"

Yep, I was right. Jason has no idea I'm standing behind him.

Curtis spots me as he turns away from the barn to start walking.

"Um, Jason?" I hesitate. "Um, I'm not in the house. I'm standing behind you. Please don't be mad. I wanted to check on my brother."

Jason turns around to face me with a smile. "Of course you did. I know how tight you two are and I know you worry about your brother, so it doesn't surprise me you were standing there, but, Anna, Jessica could have used your help setting the table."

Jason turns sideways and walks to the beach by the lake. Curtis and I stand motionless trying to figure out what he is doing. Jason picks up a rock and holds it in his hand like he is watching an ant crawl around, which is something I like to do. Then without warning, the rock flies across the water. It skips four times.

"What?" my brother yells. "Jason, you just skipped a rock four times. My sister Anna can't even do that."

Jeez, thanks, Curtis, for blowing me in.

"I'm not too bad at it, Curtis. Like you, I like to see how many times I can skip a rock. How about we do this together later?" Jason then turns toward the water as if looking for something and then turns back to face us. "Better yet, how about now?"

Curtis runs toward him, and I stand still like I'm watching a movie. This is the first time someone else has thrown a rock with my brother other than me. I feel sad but happy at the same time. I'm sad he found someone else to throw with him, but happy that maybe he'll begin to like living here since Jason throws rocks too.

Jason hollers over the waves of water. "Anna! How about you get in the house and help Jessica? Tell her we will be in shortly." With that, he turns and throws another rock with Curtis.

I don't want to leave my brother with Jason. But maybe Curtis needs to spend some time with somebody besides me so he can, maybe, start to like it here. That way, I won't have to feel so guilty for making him leave the place he liked way more than I did.

As I open the front door, I catch a glimpse of Jason and Curtis still standing by the water. My brother's laughter echoes across the yard and slams right into me. *Please, Jesus, let my brother be happy.*

"Jason, is that you? I could use your help here getting some stuff on the table so the kids can get ready to eat." Jessica's voice sings from the kitchen to the foyer. She always sounds happy, even when she asks someone to do something for her. She's nothing like my other foster mothers. Though Sue, my last foster mother, was always nice to me, it was because she wanted to get me alone in her bedroom. So far, Jessica doesn't want anything from me, or at least she hasn't yet. My stomach hurts again, and I wring my hands together like I'm washing them in the sink.

47

I hope she doesn't ever want anything from me, like secret girl time. I hope.

I make my way under the archway into the kitchen. "Hey, Jessica, it's me. Jason and Curtis are out by the lake throwing rocks, and he wanted me to come in to see if you need some help with setting the table."

Even while cooking dinner, she has tight pants on, her hair is done, and her face looks like one of those tall, skinny dolls that my friends would bring to school in first grade. She turns and, with her hand in an oven mitt, waves it for me to come to her.

"Why are they doing that when it's time for dinner? Ugh. I worked hard on this lasagna, and they should be in here eating it."

I try to get rid of the lump in my throat. "Um… Jessica? My brother is having a hard time with the idea of eating lasagna because, you see, at our last foster home, our mom made it all the time because it's Curtis's favorite meal. I don't want to make you feel sad, Jessica, but I think I should tell you that Curtis is really upset because he's here. He wants to go back to our last mom. He was really close to her."

"That makes sense. It explains why he's so angry right now. Maybe that is why he's fighting with you."

I didn't think about it before, but maybe Jessica is right because my brother has never attacked me and he's definitely never hit me before, not like he did today. So maybe that's what it is all about. Maybe it's not because I wouldn't do alone time with our last foster mom after all. Maybe he's simply mad at me because he didn't want to leave.

Jessica puts her hand on my shoulder. "This isn't your fault, little lady. Your brother is mad, and it's not about something you did to him. Sometimes, when people feel strong emotions, they come out in different ways. Some people worry, some get depressed, some get scared, and others get angry. I bet your brother feels his emotions by getting angry."

Jessica smiles, which makes me feel good, like when I'm eating my favorite ice cream cone, mint chocolate chip.

"Let's get this table set so we can eat before midnight. Who knows how long those two will be outside?"

***

Jason and Curtis finally come inside just as it is getting dark. Jessica and I have already eaten our lasagna and are cleaning up the dishes. "I thought maybe you boys planned on staying out there all night playing with those rocks." Jessica giggles as she glances at Jason.

"Hmm. That's an interesting thought, honey." Jason grabs two bowls, a box of cereal, and milk. He sets them on the table. "What do you think about that idea, Curtis? Maybe you and I should plan to have a camp-out. We can take pillows and blankets and sleep on the boat." He puts his hand on Curtis' shoulder. "We could even skip rocks in the dark and see if we can hear them fall into the water. I think it's a fantastic idea; what about you?"

Curtis sits down and opens the cereal. "It does sound great. I can't wait." He giggles. "I've never slept on a boat, and I've definitely never thrown rocks at nighttime. Can we please do that, Jason? That'd be so cool." My brother wiggles in his chair and Jason's hand falls off his shoulder.

"I wouldn't have asked if I didn't think we could. So, how about, after we eat our cereal, we get our stuff and have a guys' night on the boat?" Jason winks at his wife.

"Well, honey, it looks like you and Anna are having girl time tonight 'cause the boys are gonna be sleeping out on the boat like big men." Jason puts his hands on the waistband of his pants and acts like he's pulling them up while marching around the table as Jessica laughs.

Uh oh… *girls' night.* I feel sick to my stomach. I wanna puke right here in the sink while I'm rinsing dishes. I gotta come up with something fast. I don't want to have a girls' night. I *never* wanna have girls' night again ever.

Curtis slurps his cornflakes, but I can't get distracted right now. I have to come up with a reason for why I don't want to have girl time. "Um… Jessica? I… um… hafta… um… finish unpacking my bag, so, I… um… really don't want to have girl time tonight. But thanks anyway."

Jessica tilts her head and puts a hand on her hip. "Are you sure? We can have popcorn and soda, and watch something on TV."

"Jessica, are you gonna buy me anything for girls' night?"

She looks down at me as she moves the pot from her side of the sink to mine. "Honey, why would I buy you a present for girl's night? I mean, don't get me wrong, there may be times that I buy presents for you and your brother."

She has her eyes squished together like she's trying to figure out something, or she's trying to fix a puzzle. Her gaze doesn't move off me.

"Did you have girl time before at your old foster home?"

I say nothing and rinse the dish before I put it on the rack on the black, shiny countertop.

"Anna, sweetheart, did you have girl time at your old foster home?"

"Hey buddy," Jason says, scraping his chair across the floor. "Why don't you and I go out on the back porch with our cereal and let the girls have some time so they can talk."

Almost instantly, Jason and Curtis are gone.

"Anna, did your last foster mother give you presents every time you had girl time?"

Slowly, I nod.

"Did you like the presents she bought for you?"

"Sometimes," I whisper.

Jessica isn't doing the dishes anymore. Instead, she watches me before speaking again. "Anna, can I ask you another question?"

I nod.

"Did your old foster mother make you do things when she bought you presents?"

"Huh?" I know what Jessica is asking, but I'm not going to tell her what Sue did to me because she'll think I'm dirty and gross. And she might make me leave because she might think I'm a bad kid for doing that.

But I have to say something because she's still looking at me. "Um. She would, um… she would… um… tell me she bought me presents because I would help her with the house."

Jessica smiles. "Well, that's nice. Sometimes, it's nice to get presents when you do something in the house to help. What did she buy your brother for helping?"

Jessica's eyes go back to being scrunched together. Does she know something?

"Um… I don't know. I don't think so. She bought us a bunch of things for Christmas, but I never saw her buy Curtis anything special like she did me every Wednesday."

Jessica goes back to cleaning a glass while talking to me. "Every Wednesday, huh? What was so special about every Wednesday?" She hands me the glass. "Be careful with that, okay? It could be slippery, and I don't want it to fall into the sink and break. You could get hurt."

I put two hands on the glass cup, then dip it under the water.

"So, what was so special about Wednesdays?" She doesn't stop wiping the plate with green swirls all over it.

"Well, Wednesdays were the night that Allan would work so he wasn't at home. Mom always chose that night for special girl time." I set the glass in the strainer.

"*Special* girl time? Is that what she called it?"

Oh no. I freeze. Maybe I told Jessica too much. She knows now, and she's going to say something to our caseworker. Then our caseworker is going to say something to me. Oh no. What have I done?

"Uh… I don't know what you're talking about. I didn't mean to say girl *time*. I meant to say girls' *night*." I hope Jessica believes me.

"Anna, if you ever want to talk about anything, I am here to listen. You can tell me anything. If anybody has hurt you in any kind of way you can tell me, okay?"

She hands me a plate and I dunk it into the water. "Uh, sure." If only she knew I was completely lying to her right now because I am *never* going to tell anybody ever again what anybody does to me. After all, no matter what I say, nobody helps me, and all it does is hurt my brother by making us move.

I put the last plate on the counter after rinsing it, then drain the water out of the sink.

"Okay, Anna, you're free to go upstairs to finish unpacking your bag before it's time for bed. I can get the rest of this kitchen cleaned up. Thank you for your help. It's nice having someone in the kitchen with me on the nights that I choose to cook." Jessica laughs a little bit. "You will come to see that I don't spend much time in this kitchen. Usually, it's Jason who does most of the cooking."

I turn to go upstairs, but Jessica grabs my hand. "Anna, you can talk to me if your foster mother or anyone else did something to you. I won't tell anyone."

Jessica looks like she has a tear in her eye and I really wish I could tell her everything. All about Derek hurting my girl parts in my first foster home and how my last foster mother made me suck on her boobies like I was a baby. And how my birth mother gave me away and played awful games to hurt me.

I wish I could tell her all of that—but what difference would it make? How could she make any of it better? How could she ever protect me from anything like it from happening again? I mean, she's nice, but she's no one to me. She's just another mother.

51

"Thanks. I'm okay." With that, I turn around and head upstairs to go into my room and unpack my stuff. To make this place my new home for real.

The garbage bag crinkles as I reach inside. I touch something sharp and pointy.

What can that be? I don't remember packing anything like tha…

Oh.

It's the glass bird.

Chapter 7
Broken Mirror

"No, I don't want to do girl time. No, you cannot make me do that to your boobies anymore. I'm not a baby.

No! Stop.

I don't want to lie down on the bed with you. You're gross and sweaty. Leave me alone. Leave me alone."

I snap out of my make-believe mind when I hear my goat friends making noise in their pen. But it wasn't make-believe; it was real. It really happened to me.

My last foster mother, Sue, made me do that to her. I am so dirty and gross now. I can never tell anyone. Never.

I rub my nose over and over again. I swear I can still smell her sweaty skin. That smell seems to have burnt itself inside my nose. I stare at the pink, glass bird in my hand as if I am waiting for it to come alive and fly around my room.

Sue gave me this bird. She took it off the Christmas tree.

The first Christmas tree I'd ever seen.

The first Christmas tree I've ever had.

She'd made me feel like no one could ever hurt me again—and definitely not her.

But she'd lied.

The bird came to life and flew right into my dresser mirror.

Footsteps pound up the stairs and down the hallway to my room, and the door gets flung open like a tornado's blasting through.

"Anna?"

Jessica's in here with me, but I can hardly see her since everything's blurry.

"What happened?" Jessica puts her hands up. "Anna, don't move. You'll cut your feet." She runs to the doorway. "Jason, can you get gloves on and grab the vacuum so we can clean up this glass? It's all over the place."

I can't move. It's not that I don't want to move; I can't. It's like everything is happening all around me but I'm not here.

But I am. Jason carries me to the bed.

"She's as stiff as a board," Jason says. He sits me down on my bed. I feel paralyzed.

"Jason, while you're downstairs, please grab my penlight so I can check her eyes."

I can hear everything they're saying, but I can't move.

"Anna, don't be afraid. I know you can hear me. I know you feel like nothing on your body works right now, but it does. It's just your mind freezing up. You're in shock. I'm going to wrap this blanket around you. If you can hear me, blink your eyes."

I do as she says.

"Phew, good." She drapes the blanket over my shoulders. "You are going to be okay. Can I touch your back? Blink twice if I can."

I don't want her touching me. I scream in my head. *I don't want anyone to touch me!* So I don't blink my eyes.

"Anna, can I touch you? Blink twice for yes and once for no."

I blink once.

"Okay, honey, I won't touch you. Can I hold your hand? Blink twice for yes and once for no."

I blink twice.

Within seconds, Jessica has her hand on mine. "I hear the goats have taken a liking to you, especially Sticks. I was told she even cuddled with you in the barn." She squeezes my hand a little harder. "I need you to stay focused on my voice. I am going to count, and in your head, I want you to count with me. Are you ready? Here we go. One... two... three..."

Though I still can't move any part of my body, I start counting with her. With each number, I feel parts of my body again. No matter the number, though, I can't get Sue's sweaty, gross-smelling skin out of my nose.

"Seven... eight. Good job, Anna." Jessica talks as slow as the tick-tock sound from the grandfather clock in the dining room.

"Give her this." Curtis walks in and puts something on my lap. "Here you go, Anna. Your doll."

Her yarn hair tickles my arm. *Finally,* I can breathe and move again.

"There you are, Anna." Jessica tries to reassure me. Though she smiles and talks slowly with me, her eyes are wide open and burn a hole through me because she doesn't look away. "Don't be afraid. Sometimes, when people get really scared, they can freeze, like you did just now, but you're okay."

Though I'm not frozen anymore, I don't feel so good.

"What happened to the mirror?"

Jessica doesn't sound mad at all.

I spot the bird on the floor surrounded by the broken glass.

Jessica points at it. "Is that making you upset?"

I'm going to puke. I shrug the blanket from my shoulders. My body shakes, and before I can stop it, I throw up my entire dinner all over the pink carpet in my bedroom.

Jason comes back into the room. "Get a bucket or towels fast." Jessica hollers while she moves my hair out of my face.

I can't stop throwing up. More and more puke comes flying out of my mouth.

Jessica sits beside me, holding my hair back as I bend over, heaving until there's nothing left, though my body doesn't stop trying.

"Jason! Hurry up! She's still throwing up," Jessica yells. That's the loudest I've heard her talk so far since I've lived here.

Jason comes running back into the room and tosses some towels to Jessica.

"She's not stopping. There cannot be anything left inside of her little belly to throw up." Jessica puts her hand on my back. "Calm down, sweetheart. Try to take a breath so your body stops convulsing."

I can't. My stomach won't listen to my brain.

"C'mon. Anna, breathe. I'm right here next to you. You are not in trouble, and we can get another mirror to replace that one. It's not a big deal. Is this why you're so upset? What happened, Anna? What happened to the mirror?"

She stands up and grabs the bird from the middle of the floor. "I'm guessing this belongs to you?"

I stare at it and my stomach churns again. "Get it away from me! I don't want it!" I gag and my throat hurts, but I hafta tell her to get rid of it. "Get it away from me! I don't want it!"

Jessica sits back on the bed next to me. "Your eyes are enormous, honey. What's going on? Let me help you. Let me in."

Jason walks back into the room with a bucket and a towel.

"Jason, get rid of this bird."

He takes it. "It's pretty, Anna. Are you sure you want me to throw it away?"

For the first time, I see Jessica shoot Jason a mad look. Her eyes scrunch together, and so do her lips. "Get rid of the bird, please."

"Okay, honey, consider it gone." He turns to leave with the bird in his hand. He stops in the doorway where Curtis stands. "Hey buddy, I know you're worried about your sister, but how about you and I go into your bedroom? We can play a game or watch some TV while Jessica and your sister have some time alone to talk. Anna is clearly upset by something, and maybe she just needs a girl to help her."

"Is my sister okay? Is she hurt? Does she have to go to the hospital? I see the broken glass. Are you sure she didn't cut herself?"

"She didn't get cut and she doesn't need to go to the emergency room. Let's leave Jessica alone with her so she can help. Remember, Jessica is a doctor. Doctors can help everyone. She's in good hands, bud." Jason ruffles Curtis' hair and then points to my bedroom floor.

"I know it's scary looking at the broken glass all over her bedroom, but your sister didn't cut herself.

"Why is she throwing up?" I hear my brother mumble as I hold my stomach in pain.

"She's just throwing up because something must have upset her belly. She'll be okay. But it won't help your sister if you and I stand around and watch her, especially since she doesn't feel good. Let's give her some space, bud."

With that, Curtis disappears out of my doorway.

Jessica moves closer to me. Our legs touch. "Anna, talk to me. I want to help you. What is it about that bird that made you so upset?"

I don't want to talk about the bird.

"Honey, can I ask you a question?"

When she asks me if she can ask me a question, it's probably about Sue.

I nod.

"Did your last foster mother give you that bird?"

All the air leaves my lungs and I can't breathe again.

She grabs my hand. "Honey, I am not upset with you. I want to help you. You can tell me anything and I won't say anything to anybody. Did Sue give you that bird in the last foster home? Was that one of your gifts during girl time?"

I don't jerk my hand away from Jessica because she's not scary. I think she's trying to help, but I've learned nobody can really help me. The question she's asking always ends badly for Curtis and me.

"Anna, did Sue give you that bird?"

I breathe in as much air as I can and nod.

"Honey." Jessica squeezes my hand. "Did she give you that bird during girl time?"

I shake my head. "No. Sue gave me the bird off the Christmas tree the first night we were in their house. We never had a Christmas before and that was the first time we ever saw a Christmas tree. I forgot all about it until I pulled it out of my garbage bag."

"Oh, so did you get to pack your clothes?"

I shake my head.

"So, you had no idea the bird was in your garbage bag." Jessica goes back to whispering again.

"No." I speak as quietly as possible.

"I'm guessing from your reaction that you didn't want to bring the bird with you." Her eyes narrow and she gets a big wrinkle between them.

I nod.

"I'm sorry. Clearly the bird upsets you and you were shocked when you saw it was in your bag. Did the bird make you feel angry?"

I nod again. It reminds me of the promises that Sue broke. She told me that she would not hurt me. She said we would be safe at her house. The woman acted like she loved me and wanted me as her daughter.

All of it was lies.

And she is the one who hurt me.

That's what I see when I look at the bird. All lies. I rub my hands together and wiggle back and forth sitting on the bed. I want to run away from Jessica's questions, but I can't because there is glass all over my floor and Jessica is sitting so close to me. I can smell her breath and it smells like mint.

I wish she would stop talking and asking me questions. I wish she would leave me alone.

"Anna, did Sue hurt you?" She sounds like Daddy in my first foster home when he asked me if Derek had hurt me.

I'm back in the garage sitting on Daddy's lap. I can smell the gasoline in the containers. I can smell his cologne. That day changed my life. When I told him the truth, I lost Daddy forever.

I don't want to move and I *can't* move Curtis again. My tears burn the very whites of my eyes. I won't cry. I won't let Jessica see me cry. The memories of Daddy still torture me and send shooting pain through every bone in my body. How can I tell her the truth? It only comes with being moved and making people mad. Daddy said I had to leave because he couldn't keep me safe. Sue got mad at me when I told her I didn't want secret girl time anymore.

If I tell this nice family what Sue did, they could tell Curtis. Mrs. Alex would find out and Jessica will want me to move. If Curtis finds out that I said something bad about Sue, he would definitely not believe me. He would hate me.

No way! I can*not* tell her that Sue hurt me. I can't.

I shake my head.

Jessica says nothing at first. She leans closer to me and it feels like her lips could touch my cheek if she puckered. "Anna, are you sure that Sue didn't do anything to hurt you? If you don't want to tell me anything, I want to make sure you know you can always tell me another time."

How could Sue hurt me like she did? She told me I would be safe at her house—and then lied to me. I *wasn't* safe at her house. *She* hurt me.

Tears fill my eyes, waiting for the opportunity to drop down my face. I turn my head to the side to hide from Jessica.

"Did you throw that bird across the room and that's what happened when it smashed into the mirror?" Jessica turns her head away from me to look at the broken mirror glass all over my floor.

I nod. "I'm sorry."

"I don't think it's a good idea for you to stay in your room because we really have to clean up this glass so you don't get hurt. And, to be honest, it's really stinky in here. What do you think about going outside and spending some time by the lake or in the barn? I need to clean this up for you."

I nod. "Okay and I'm really sorry I didn't mean to break the mirror on the pretty dresser."

Jessica stands up at the end of my bed, holding her hand out to me. "Follow me so you don't step on any glass. I don't want to have to dig glass out of your foot."

I take my doll off my lap and lay her on the bed before following Jessica. I don't want to let go of her hand because she's nice. But... so was Sue.

I drop Jessica's hand anyway. Because maybe... no one is safe.

Chapter 8
A New Baby

As I get close to the lake, I see Curtis and Jason throwing more rocks.

"I beat you again, Jason. You suck." Curtis dances around.

He must've beaten Jason again. One thing I can say about my brother is that no one can beat him at rock-skipping. I've been trying to do that for as long as I can remember, and it hasn't happened yet.

Jason sees me. "Anna, come here. I want to show you something."

He runs to me in a full sprint. Does that man ever walk anywhere? Within seconds, Jason reaches the goat pen. "Are you okay, sweetheart? Is your stomach feeling better?"

I don't feel like talking so I nod.

He opens the goat pen with a huge smile on his face. "Boy, do I have something to show you."

"Holy cow. What is that? She's beautiful. Can I touch her?" I walk toward the little black thing curled up in the hay.

"Of course you can touch her, but be careful because she might be scared. She's just a baby," Jason whispers to me.

"Where did you get this baby goat? How long has she been here?" I stand by the door, hoping he says I can sit by her and rub her fur.

"Go ahead and sit with her if you want."

I waste no time, hoping Jason doesn't change his mind. I open the pen door slowly but its squeak echoes throughout the barn. The hay crunches under my tip toes as I walk to the fur ball with hooves.

I sit beside her and rub her belly. She doesn't move. She's not afraid of me. This little baby hasn't learned yet that big people can be dangerous and hurt them. I'm not a big person, but I am big compared to this baby. I know how big people can hurt kids. I'll protect this baby goat so no one hurts it, not even the other barn animals.

"Does she have a name?" I scratch between its ears, hoping the baby likes it.

Curtis comes running into the barn. "What's going on in there? Why isn't anybody throwing rocks with me anymore?"

"It's nearly dusk outside so how can you see how far the rocks are going?" Jason pats Curtis on the shoulder. "Plus, see our new baby goat? Go on in with your sister to see her."

Curtis isn't really into animals like I am, so I'm not surprised when he shakes his head.

"Nah, I'm gonna go back to throwing rocks." He heads back out.

"Can I name her? Can I?" I keep asking until Jason stops picking up poop and talks to me.

"Come to think of it, Jessica already gave her a name. But maybe we can give her two names."

"What name did Jessica give her?" I don't look at Jason because I'm too busy rubbing the baby goat's black fur. It's so dark it seems like the middle of the night.

"I think Jessica wants to call her Betty."

"Betty? Isn't that a name for a grown up?"

Jason laughs. "Yeah, I guess you could say that, but Jessica wants to call her Betty. So, Betty it will be. However, why don't we make Betty her last name, and you can give her another name."

Jason is full of great ideas for a grown-up. This baby goat will be like me. When I was born, my birth mother didn't know what to name me. So, she gave me four first names, Anna Sarah Bailey Snow, though I only go by Anna Snow.

I went by Sarah Bailey in my first foster home. I'm glad I don't have to use that anymore. Whenever I hear someone say Sarah, it brings back memories of my first foster mother holding my hands under hot water to punish me. *"You make me do this Sarah. If you weren't so bad."* I quiver at the memory of her and the pain in my hands. I will never go by Sarah Bailey again because it makes me hurt.

"Can I call her Black Betty because her fur is so black?"

"Sure. That's a great idea. Black Betty it is."

I lean down, putting my head closer to her. "Hello, Black Betty. I'm gonna feed you and take care of you. I'm gonna make sure that Twinkles and Sticks are nice, too."

"Anna, do you wanna feed her?"

"Can I?"

"Yep. Give me a few minutes to get her food ready."

I sit and continue to whisper to Black Betty as I pet her fur. I always feel safer with animals. I love this goat so much I fear my heart will burst.

Within a few minutes, I hear footsteps and then see Jason, who holds a giant bottle up in the air.

"She drinks from a bottle like human babies do?"

"This one does. She lost her mother too early so we're gonna bottle feed her for a little while. Let me show you how to do it and then you can take over." Jason enters the pen and holds the bottle above her head.

Within seconds, Black Betty is pushing on the bottle with her mouth.

"Do you think you can do this?"

"Sure can." I jump up fast to grab the bottle from Jason.

"Keep it up high so she has to extend her neck upward a little. You want to make the feeding as close to natural as possible."

I nod as Jason walks away, feeling proud of being trusted to feed Black Betty. She must be hungry because drinks and drinks and drinks.

After she's done, I lose track of time. I spend most of the evening making Black Betty a hay bed. I clean up her poop and feed her some more of her bottle. She's really like my little baby. When I walk around her pen, Black Betty follows me saying, *"Mahhhm.* It sounds like she is saying *mom. I* am her foster mom now.

Twinkles and Sticks don't leave the outside of her pen and make the same *mahhhm* sounds to this little girl.

I have another new friend here, in my new foster home. Big people hurt me. Animals don't.

Jason comes back in after I'm all done and the goat is sleeping by my feet. "How's it going in there? Do you need any help?"

"Nope, I got it. I love this. Can I feed her every day?"

"Sure you can, that will help me out. I'll get you up in the morning. We have to get ready to head back to the house."

"She drank the whole thing."

"Perfect. Go ahead and leave the bottle in the bulk tank sink and I'll clean it later."

I do as he says. Once I brush the hay off of me, I give Black Betty a kiss goodnight.

Jason waits for me, but seems ready to go. "It's time to come into the house and get ready to go to bed. Jessica has cleaned up your room and shampooed your carpet, so it may be wet in one area. Just go ahead and walk around it."

"Could I sleep in the barn tonight with Black Betty and the other goats? I can sleep right here." I pat the hay mound I built. "I used to sleep with Thunder at my old foster home, so this isn't new. And the hay will keep me warm. If I need anything, you and Curtis are just outside in the boat, right?" I cross my fingers he'll say yes.

"Sorry, Anna, but there's no way Jessica's going to allow that to happen. She thinks sleep is super important, so the best place for you to get your rest is going to be in your bed."

Darn it. I cross my arms and walk to the pen door.

Meow. I pick up Lucky, who is rubbing against my leg. "Can I take Lucky in the house? I'll let her sleep with me in my bedroom. I bet she's lonely because all her brothers and sisters left today." I kiss her head.

"Let me share this with you." Jason's voice sounds like he ate a frog. "You can love on all the animals you want in the barn, but none of them should ever find their way inside the house." The only animal Jessica let in the house was our Irish Wolfhound Dughal. No other animals are allowed in the house since he died." He opens the pen door waving his hand at me.

"What's an Irish Wolfhound?"

His eyes get big. "You've never seen a picture of an Irish

Wolfhound? They are gigantic dogs, sometimes as tall as a small pony. That was how tall Jessica's Dughal was."

"What happened to him, Jason? How did he die?"

Jason stops and stands in front of me. His shoulders droop as if he's carrying something heavy on them. "Well… his lungs stopped working and he couldn't breathe. So, we had to take him to the vet and there was nothing they could do for him. They gave him medicine to help him fall asleep forever." Jason sniffles. "I don't talk about him much because it still makes Jessica sad, even though it's been a year since we lost him."

"I know what that feels like." I stop talking as Jason sits on a hay bale and motions for me to sit next to him. "I'm still sad about losing my daddy and having to leave Momma Cat and Lucky behind in my first foster home. Then I had to leave my friends and Thunder in the last place I lived, along with all the friends I made at school and my teachers."

I stop and take a deep breath. "It's like everyone and everything dies all at once because you can never see them again when you're a foster kid. They all die. Your foster parents, your foster sisters or brothers, your school, your teachers, your friends at school, your friends that live by you, your pets, your church, and sometimes, I feel like I die with them too. Every time we have to go someplace new, it's like everyone and everything disappears and I have to start all over in another world." This time, I feel the lump. I swallow as much as I can to hold it back.

Jason sniffles. "Um..I'm sorry, Anna. I can't even begin to imagine what that feels like for you."

I look up. Jason wipes a tear on his cheek with his hand. "It's sad." I choke.

"I'm sure it is," Jason whispers.

Meow. Lucky rubs up against my leg and I pick her up to bury my face in her fur. Maybe I can put my head down and hide my tears in her black fur like I do in the material of my doll.

"Sorry, Lucky, I asked, but you can't come in." I kiss her head. "I'll come visit you tomorrow." I put her back down.

Lucky must be super sad. I can't imagine how I'd feel if I didn't have my brother with me. I would die without Curtis.

"Let's get going in the house, little lady, before Jessica yells at us."

He laughs, and so do I, because I could never see Jessica yelling at anyone. She's too busy being gross by kissing Jason all the time. I giggle a little more at the thought.

I stand up and brush the hay off me. "Goodnight, Black Betty. Goodnight, Sticks. Goodnight, Twinkles. Goodnight, Lucky."

When I leave the barn, Curtis is standing by the water, throwing rocks in the dark. The only light he has is the pole light between the dock and the boat barn. No way can he see the rock go across the water. It's too dark to see out in the lake.

Jason yells loudly, above the sound of the water. "Curtis, it's time for you and I to climb into the boat to get ready for bed."

My brother yells, "Nope! I'm not going to do that. It's not dark out, so I don't have to go to bed."

My head whips around fast. Wow. I then look at Jason. We both stand staring at my brother. Neither of us says anything.

"Excuse me? *What* did you say, Curtis?"

"I said that I'm not going in the boat. I'm gonna stay out here and I'm gonna throw rocks. I don't want to sleep in your stupid boat anyway," my brother hollers back.

I've never heard him talk to anybody like that, ever.

"Anna, head into the house. Jessica's waiting for you because she wants to talk to you before you go to bed. I'll take care of your brother."

"Jason, maybe you should be the one to go in the house. My brother will listen to me more than he will to you right now. I can get my brother to go inside."

Jason stares at me for a second. "I think it's better if I talk with Curtis, but thank you for trying to help. Jessica's waiting on you. I've got this." Jason walks across the yard toward my brother.

I decide to do as Jason asks and head back to the house. The last time Curtis was this mad he attacked me. I know Jason won't hurt him like maybe other foster parents would have.

"Can you come here for a second, please?" Jessica asks when I walk into the kitchen. She holds up a cup. "I like to have tea at night before I go to sleep because it makes it easier for me to calm down, and it stops my mind from thinking. Do you ever feel like your mind is always thinking?"

I'm more worried about my brother than my mind, but since I don't want to be rude, I nod. "Yes. My mind doesn't stop. I'm always thinking about something. Makes it hard for me to do my math in school because I don't want to think about four plus four. I wanna think about jumping rope during recess, instead."

"I get that. I liked to jump rope, too, when I was in school." Jessica takes a sip, and her eyes meet mine. "Do you remember when I asked if Sue hurt you at your last foster home?"

Ugh. I feel like Jessica just punched me and knocked my air out. Every time she asks me about Sue, I feel this way. I stand by the table and stare at my feet.

"I get the feeling that there's something you don't want to tell me. Remember… I'm just here to help you. If there's anything I can do, please let me know."

I stare at my shoes, realizing I never took them off when I came into the house. I hope Jessica doesn't notice.

"Anna, do you want to tell me anything?"

I shake my head. "No. There's nothing I want to tell you except that I'm tired and ready to go to bed." I yawn and hope my fake yawn works.

Jessica takes a deep breath. "All right, honey, I can see that you're tired. Go ahead and get your pajamas on. I cleaned your bedroom. Just watch for places in the carpet that might still be wet," she said, repeating what Jason has already told me. "I'll see you in the morning for breakfast." She raises her cup to me.

"Okay," I mumble.

"Goodnight. Have a good night's sleep, Anna."

I leave quickly, before Jessica changes her mind and wants to ask me more questions. I've had enough of talking about Sue and the bird today. I just don't wanna talk about them anymore.

Once upstairs, I brush my teeth and change into my pajamas. As I pull back my comfy blanket, I hear my brother stomping up the steps, screaming.

"I'm not going to bed and you're not my mom so you can't make me! You're just a stupid foster parent and I don't care! I don't want to sleep in your stupid boat. And… don't follow me."

"Hey, bud," Jason says. Amazingly, he's not yelling back at Curtis. "It's time for bed, and no matter how mad you get or how much you throw a fit, it's not going to change a thing. It's 9:30, and I even let you stay up a little later than your sister, so, be as mad as you want as long as you're in your bed. If you calm down and decide you want to sleep in the boat, let me know. Good night, Curtis."

Then I hear my brother's howling scream. "I hate you, and I don't want to be here." He slams his bedroom door, shaking the whole house.

I jump out of bed to go to my brother. When I reach my door, I see Jason leaning against Curtis' closed door. I guess the outburst stopped him from leaving. I stay in my room, but try to watch through the three inches my door hangs open.

"Curtis, can I come in to talk with you?" Jason says.

"No," he screams. "Get away from me. I hate you and I want to go home. I want to go back to my mom. I don't want to be here."

"Curtis, buddy. I know you want to go back to your mom and I wish I could make that happen for you, but I can't. You have to be here." Jason sounds kind.

"I want to call her," Curtis screams. He sounds like a wild animal. "I want to call my mom."

Before Jason answers him, I already know the answer. In my last foster home, I asked Sue if I could call Daddy all the time. She told me it wasn't allowed, but it didn't stop me from asking. Though I know he didn't die, just like I told Jason, it felt like it. The 'no' always made me cry harder. Foster kids should be allowed to visit their old families if they want to. It's a dumb rule that we can't ever call them again.

Really stupid.

When I get bigger, I'm going to change that rule and make sure that all foster kids can call their old families if they want to. Yup, that's what I'm gonna do.

"I'm sorry, Curtis. You aren't able to do that. When you're in foster care, they don't allow you to call anyone in your old foster home. I don't like that either, and I think it's wrong, but those are the rules." Jason's voice is getting louder, but he's not yelling.

"Please, Jason, can't you take me to my mom? Please, Jason."

Jason turns his head toward my door, and I step back into the darkness of my room so he can't see me standing there. I don't want to get in trouble for not being in my bed. After a quiet, tense minute, I step back up, careful to stay in the dark, so I can watch again.

Jason is crying. He wipes his face. "I'm sorry. I wish I could help you." Jason has his hand on the door.

My brother says nothing, and the room goes quiet.

Jason finally leaves.

I wait 'til I hear him talking to Jessica downstairs before I slip out of my room and go to my brother's door.

"Curtis, it's me. Anna." No sound comes from his room. I wait, hoping he changes his mind... but he doesn't.

I tiptoe back to my room, defeated. The comforter on my bed is fluffy and comfortable as I wrap it around my neck. I close my eyes.

Jesus. I'm worried about my brother. He's never been so mad. Please help him, Jesus. I know he misses Sue, but I don't think Curtis knows what she did to me. If he knew, I don't think he'd miss her so much. Thank you for giving me Jason and Jessica. They seem friendly. And thanks for bringing Black Betty to my new house. I can't wait to get to know her and feed her again. I'm sorry, Jesus, but I haven't been to your house lately. I'll talk to my foster parents tomorrow to see if they can take me to your house. It's only been two days since we've been here, and it's starting to get easier already. Thank you for listening to me, Jesus. Thank you for always being there. Amen and goodnight, Jesus.

Chapter 9
The Dock

"Good morning, Anna. Rise and shine. It's July 15th and this is the first day of swim lessons."

I sit up quickly when I hear Jason's voice. I've been waiting for over a month for this week to get here. I circled the date on the calendar in the kitchen. He told me about swimming lessons the first few days when we arrived here, so I've been waiting since the end of May. Finally, it's July and I can learn to swim.

I dig the sand out of the corner of my eyes. Jessica comes into focus. "Wow, I thought you were Jason."

Jessica puts a fist in the air like she wants to fight me and giggles. "I sound like a man, do I?"

"No, not at all."

"Honey, you've been with us now for almost two months. Why

don't you call me Jess? My mother is the only one who calls me Jessica. She's no longer with us and is in heaven now."

"I'm sorry you lost your mother. I lost my mother too when I was a baby. But... I should say, she gave me away because she didn't want me. So, I guess I didn't really lose her like you did your mother."

"Her loss, Anna. You're a great young lady. Don't ever blame yourself for what your birth mother was not able to do. It's her fault she couldn't care for you and *not* yours."

She bends over and gets close to my face, moving my hair with her fingertips, tucking it behind my ears. She does that a lot, and it reminds me of Daddy because he used to do the same thing.

"Let me see those beautiful, dark eyes." She stands back up and puts her hands on her hips. I look up at her. "Do you hear me? Don't ever blame yourself. It's her loss."

Jessica, I mean Jess, is right. It's not my fault and I have to stop thinking that it is. I've heard that a lot so it must be true. My birth mother will regret it one day, giving me away like I was trash. I'll show her. Someday everyone will know me. When she wants to get to know me, I'm going to tell her... no thank you.

My stomach hurts for a second. I feel sad at that thought. It's like there's two of me in my mind. One crying out for my birth mother, and the other one who is strong and says all the things I was just thinking.

I wonder if my birth mother thinks of me. I wond—

"I got you this." I almost fall backward onto my comforter when Jessica sits on my bed. She holds up a purple bathing suit. Thankfully, it's not pink. Curtis told Jessica weeks ago that I didn't like pink during one of his screaming fits.

I've gotten used to them now... his fits. When I hear them, I still cry, but I know that I can't help him. The few times I tried, we ended up fighting, and Curtis got grounded. So, I learned weeks ago it's better for Jessica or Jason to help him because when I try, it seems to make him angrier and he gets into more trouble. This makes me cry harder when I hear him screaming in his room.

Jess tells me I should go to the barn when Curtis has a fit. It sounds like a good idea, because I wouldn't have to hear him. But, if I did that, I'd feel like I was leaving him. So, I stay in my room listening 'til he calms down.

"Do you like it?" Jess is happy holding up the bathing suit.

70

I actually do. "Yeah, I mean, yes, I do."

"Good catch, Anna. You're sounding so proper these days." Jess's cheeks puff up big while she smiles, revealing all of her teeth.

"Get up and get around, and I can take you to the pool with me. Curtis doesn't want to take lessons. So, you will be spending a lot of time with me this week."

She holds her hand up. I've learned that Jess likes to give me high-fives when I agree to something. I like it when she does it. It makes me feel happy, like she cares. *Smack.* Our hands meet with a loud crack that rings throughout the upstairs.

She leaves my room. I like calling her Jess more than Jessica. It makes me feel closer to her, like a mom, but I don't have to call her mom. I like that.

I quickly put on my purple bathing suit. I also have a little, yellow, striped dress to go over top of it, and my yellow flip flops with a flower on top. Jessica likes to buy Curtis and me clothes and bring us home new outfits weekly.

Just as I reach the bottom step, Jess hands me a little bag and opens the front door at the same time. "Have to eat breakfast in the car so I'm not late."

I underestimated how many other kids would be there for lessons. Great. I wring my hands together as Jess parks the car. Her gaze falls to my lap. She grabs my hands.

"Don't worry. I won't let these kids be mean to you. I've got your back." Jess's smile makes me feel peaceful. This is Jess's favorite word, peaceful. I've learned so much from her since I've lived with them.

"Are you okay?" Jess's voice brings me out of my thoughts.

I nod.

"Let's go."

It didn't take long for me to learn the doggy paddle with my group of kids. I was in Jess's swim class.

"Anna, you're doing great."

A little girl with dark hair paddles by me. So far, no one has treated me badly and I hope it stays that way.

"Okay, kids. Our time is up today. So, let's get out of the water and head into the pool house to get changed. It's almost time for your parents to come for you."

Once inside the pool house, we line up in front of the bench.

"Let's count off so I know everyone is here," Jess says. We all stand with our dry clothes on. She points to each of us as we count. "What a great, first day." Jess claps her hands and the kids do the same. "I will see you guys tomorrow."

"Wow, your mom is so cool. I wish she was mine." A little girl with blonde hair stops and talks with me for a second. Before I can say anything, she turns and walks away.

I wish Jess was my mom. Why couldn't Jesus give me a mom like her? But instead I guess, he gave me a foster mom like her, so that's good.

I guess.

Jess hurries me outside so we can leave. She starts the car and makes the roof come off. I've never seen a car do that before I lived with Jess and Jason. The wind can mess up our hair as she drives, but I don't mind. It does feel kinda cool like you're flying through the air.

"Are you up for some lunch?"

Jess doesn't have to ask me twice. "Sure am." Spending time with her is my favorite thing to do. Funny, I'm never hungry when Mrs. Alex tries to stop for food, but I always love going with Jess.

The door opens to the Big M. I run to the counter. "What can I help you with, young lady?"

I back away and stand behind Jess. I hate talking to strangers.

Jess turns around. "Come on, I can show you how to order your own food." She gently puts her hand around my shoulder and guides me to the counter. "Go ahead, Anna. Tell them what you want to eat."

"I'd like a cheeseburger, french fries, and an orange soda, please." My stomach growls as the girl types in my order.

"See, honey? That wasn't so bad was it? Now you can order for yourself." Jess looks proud of me. It's a really nice feeling. I feel happy too. Now, I can swim and order my own food.

Once done, I sit back and wait for Jess to finish. It doesn't take her long.

"Yum, that was good. Let's get back home. I'm sure it's time for you to feed your goats."

***

Jason walks towards the car when he spots us pulling in. "How were swim lessons?"

"She did great, and we also had girl time and grabbed some lunch."

"Great. That sounds fun."

72

Jason is right about that. I never thought I'd like girl time, but Jess changed that for me. Her idea of girls' time doesn't hurt me. It's about us hanging out and doing something fun, like we did today.

Jess's voice changes and she sounds serious. "Did Curtis come out of his room yet?" When Jess is worried, she talks faster, like she did just now.

"No, he didn't. This fit is his longest yet." He winks at Jess.

I know what that means. These adults don't like to fight or talk about things in front of Curtis and me. Sometimes their wink means I love you and other times it means, let's talk later. I heard them one night talking in the living room when they didn't know I was sitting at the top of the stairs. I couldn't sleep. Jess said a wink would be their code to talk about something away from Curtis and me.

"I'm almost done in the barn and then I'll head in the house." Jason leans in the car and kisses Jess.

"Eww."

They both chuckle.

Mahhhm. I hear my friends, and they must be hungry. "Thanks, Jess. I had a great time." I climb out of the car so I can run to the barn.

"You might want to change out of your swim clothes before feeding the goats." Her smile always makes me feel warm inside. I know Jess really cares for me because she always does things for me. She always smiles at me.

"Can I wait till after? Please?" I put my hands together like I'm praying to Jesus.

"Fine, but change them before your piano lesson with Jason." She winks. I jump up and down, clapping my hands together.

"Okay, I will. I promise I will."

I run to the barn. "Hello Black Betty. Hey Sticks." I drop the grain in the bin.

"Anna, are you up helping me close up the barn a little tonight after piano lessons? I'm not feeling so well, so I could use your help."

I jump. I hadn't realized he had followed me to the barn. His face looks pale. "I can. Do you want to cancel piano?" I ask.

"Ah, no, that is not necessary. I enjoy the time with you on the piano. Since you started playing in the past few weeks, you've learned quickly. I heard you practicing last night. Good job." He hits my back like you would to give someone a high-five.

"Has Curtis been in his room all morning?"

Jason picks up the hay bale. "Your brother is not having a good day and refuses to come out of his room."

"Is he mad again today?" I hold my breath waiting for an answer. Curtis is mad more days than he is happy. He still cries for Sue.

"He yelled at me this morning. Maybe you can try talking to him after you finish the goats." Jason hands me the straw for the pen.

"Okay."

The goats are done now. I don't need to close Black Betty in the pen anymore because she is big enough now to walk around the big, fenced-in pasture with the other goats. She got big fast. There's nothing more to do so now I want to go see Curtis. I can't seem to calm him down when he's having a fit, but that doesn't stop me from trying.

"Bye, Jason. I'm going. My barn chores are done."

His head pops out from behind a cow he's milking as I walk by him and out of the barn. "Okay. Thank you, Anna. You do such a great job. And I'm so glad you like living with us because we like you living here very much."

"Thanks." My heart dances with joy and I skip out of the barn. "Bye cows, bye my friends, and I'll see you all later tonight."

I've never told Jason or Jess that I like to live here, but he is one hundred percent correct. The only thing missing from making it feel perfect is...

Curtis. I wish he would be happy.

Before going inside, I find my way to the dock that sways back and forth as I walk to the end. The lake waves are wild today as they slam up against the pier, making it move like sand under my feet. The boards creak and make cracking sounds like it's coming apart, but it never does. I feel the sun's warmth beat down on my face as I remove my flip flops to put my feet in the lake.

Ahh, the water feels good. I sit watching boats fly by our house with blaring music. Jess and Jason let Curtis and I do this because the lake is not deep here. If I was to jump off, I could stand up and walk back to the shore.

I don't know why I'm stalling. I meant to go right to Curtis but I didn't. Maybe because I don't understand why he's still so upset all the time. What more does Curtis want out of a foster family? They're kind, smart, and funny. We live in a huge, fancy house. They never yell or hit us. So why can't he just be happy?

Jason and Jess try everything from fishing and throwing rocks to taking him shopping for a fishing pole and army men. It only makes him happy for that day, and then it's back to screaming how much he hates them and wants to return to Sue. It makes me hate Sue even more.

Splish-Splash. I like to kick the water around at the end of the dock. I lift my head and close my eyes. For a moment, all I can hear are the seagulls making noise and the waves. When I grow up, I'm going to live on a lake. There is nothing better than feeling this—calm.

I open my eyes and hear someone scream as the roar of a boat motor fills my ears. The water skier comes closer. I can't wait to try that. Once my swim lessons are over, Jason said his friend would teach me. I can't wait.

"Anna?" Jess startles me from my thoughts of peace and fun, and I jerk my head around. She stands in the driveway by her pretty, yellow Corvette and motions for me to go to her.

I jump quickly and grab my flip flops, slipping them on as I walk. The dock makes the same noise it did in my walk out and my feet squish against the rubber of my shoes.

"Hey Jess." I wave.

"Hey, sweety, I got called into the hospital. Can you let Jason know when you see him?" She shuts her car door and starts the engine.

"Yes, I will."

I don't say *yeah* much anymore. We have to practice our grammar and how we speak. Jess and Jason both correct us so we can speak correctly.

Gonna is going.

Ain't is isn't.

Yeah is yes.

Wanna is want to, and it keeps going.

They have us talking like fancy people now, or at least, they keep correcting us so we do. It doesn't bother me when they correct me because I know they're not trying to be mean, but instead, helpful. Curtis doesn't see it the same way though, his face turns purple and most times he ignores them.

"Anna? Honey, you're daydreaming again. Did you hear what I said?"

I quickly turn my attention back to Jess. "Ah, no, I didn't. Sorry."

"Tell Jason he has to cook supper tonight. I'm not sure what time I will be home. Can you help him clean up?"

"Yes, I will."

"Thank you, honey. Have a good night." Jess waves over the top of her windshield as she pulls out of the driveway.

I'll tell Jason when he comes into the house to do piano lessons with me. Right now, it's time to check on Curtis.

Chapter 10
Piano

"Curtis? Curtis?" I yell out his name as if to warn him as I walk up the stairs. I hear nothing. "Curtis?" I knock on the door. "Curtis?"

"Yeah."

"Can I come in?"

"Yeah." The door feels like it weighs a ton as I open it. I'm not sure what I'll find on the other side.

"Curtis? Are you okay?"

He's playing on the floor with his army men and I see an empty bowl of cereal sitting next to him, along with a cup of orange juice. Leave it to Jess to make sure he eats.

"What are you doing?"

"What does it look like? I'm playing army men. I don't want to be outside today." He knocks two of his army men over with another one.

"Why are you so mad today?"

"Today? I'm mad all the time. Jason wanted me to help in the garage this morning. He said I'd like to tear apart an old car with him. He doesn't know me at all. You'd be the one to tear the car apart, not me. They like you better." He doesn't look at me as he talks.

"They don't like me better than you. It's that you don't like to spend time with them. They do a lot for you."

"If they cared at all about me, they would take me back to my Mom."

"You know that we can't do that. Just like I couldn't go back to Daddy. I remember being as sad as you are at Sue and Allen's house. All I wanted was to go back to Daddy. Remember?"

He looks up at me. "Wanna play?"

"Sure." I sit down.

"I'm always mad and sad. I don't think I know how to be happy anymore." He lines up his army men.

"You kicking my butt at throwing rocks makes you happy." I giggle.

"Yes, it does. You'll never beat me at rock skipping, no matter how hard you try." He giggles too.

"Want to try? I bet I can." I jump up and run to the door. "Come on, wussy. Are you afraid you may get beat by your sister?"

Before long, we are pushing each other out of the way as we race down the stairs. I could beat him to the door because I have a head start, but I want him to be happy so I act like I'm slower than he is on the stairs.

My plan works. My brother jumps up and down with his hands in the air at the door. "I'm the winner. Be prepared to get your butt beat at rock throwing and don't cry like a little baby." He takes his fist and rocks them back and forth in front of his eyes, pretending he is crying.

"I never cry."

I holler in the wind as I run by him. I'm off the porch when I heard the front door slam behind us. In seconds, he runs by me laughing as he heads to the lake.

***

"That was fun, wasn't it Curtis?" I sit on the sandy beach and watch him throw a few more rocks.

"Hey kids, glad to see you both out here." Jason walks to Curtis. "Holy crap. Six skips. Impressive rock skipping talent, Curtis. Maybe we can have a little competition if you'd like to." Curtis and Jason stand side by side each holding a rock.

"You're on." Curtis cheers above the water.

I wish my brother could act like this all the time. You never know from one day to another, or one minute to another, if he is going to be happy or mad.

"Jason, I forgot to tell you that Jess was called in the hospital earlier. She told me to tell you."

He turns his head. "I figured as much when I didn't see her car in the driveway. I ordered pizza for tonight. I hope that's okay with you both. I'm not hungry so it's all yours."

"Pizza. Yay." Curtis jumps up and down.

"Sounds yummy. I'm going into the house to practice the piano before our lesson."

"Sounds good, Anna. I'll be in shortly."

My fingers fall over each other as I sit down at the black, baby grand piano. Jason has taught me F.A.C.E. and E.G.B.D.F., so that's what I practice. The sounds from the piano rings through the house like I'm playing in a theater, like Jason did one time. He played on stage all by hisself while we sat in the audience and watched him. His fingers moved on a piano like a race car does on the track. It was so cool to see him up on the big stage and to know that he's teaching me to play. I live with these people. It's almost like he's famous.

"I'm here. Are you ready?" Jason comes into the piano room.

"Yes, I am. Where's Curtis?"

"He wanted to throw rocks a little more. Thanks for getting him outside."

Jason sits with me on the piano bench and continues to teach me finger positions and sharp keys. "You have the perfect hands for piano Anna. You have long fingers like me." He holds up his hand and wiggles his fingers at me.

I start playing, trying to get my fingers to hit the right keys. I concentrate so hard I almost fall off the piano seat when the doorbell goes off.

"Pizza's here. Go get your brother. We can have lessons again tomorrow night if you like. It's time to eat."

I go out the door and walk across the lawn to the lake. Curtis is sitting on the rocks playing with them. "Anna, look, I found an orange rock." It did look kinda weird sticking up as all the other rocks are black and gray.

"Cool. I'd keep it if I were you. The pizza is here. Want to come eat?" I tap his shoulder with a finger.

"Let's ra—"

Curtis is already running before he finishes what he's saying. Of course, he beats me to the house. I wish he could always be this happy. I wish.

***

I open my window to yell to my barn friends. "Hold your horses. I'm coming to get you breakfast." Black Betty is almost as big as the other two goats now. It's only mid-August and she grew a lot in the last month. I swear each week she gets bigger and bigger.

I run by Curtis's bedroom, and his door is still closed. That's not unusual anymore. He never comes out of his room unless Jason or Jessica make him. They haven't fought with him about it much this last month, but I barely saw my brother the whole month of July. I finished swimming lessons and he didn't even know it. He got mad as a hornet last week when I was allowed to go on the boat, and he wasn't. But, he's the one who refused to take lessons.

As I reach the last step, I hear Jason and Jessica singing together, and the sound rings throughout the whole house. I move fast because I don't want breakfast now. I want to spend time with my goats.

I head out the front door "Good morning, Black Betty, Twinkles, and Sticks. How did you sleep last night?" They practically dance in front of me because they've learned that I'm the one who always brings the food and water. It's not even a chore for me because I love being in the barn.

"Those goats are lucky to have you take such good care of them." Jason chuckles behind me. "As soon as you get done doing the feeding, I have some exciting news for you and your brother."

"What is it? " I jump and clap my hands.

"Have you ever been to a town fair?" Jason asks me with a gigantic smile on his face.

I stop clapping. "What's a town fair?"

Jason wrings his hands together. "A place where there are a bunch of rides, treats like cotton candy, and games you can pl—"

"Wait… is that the place with merry-go-rounds, Ferris wheels, and bumper cars? I've heard kids at school talk about how much fun those rides are."

"Yes, it is. So, why don't you go into the house to get dressed as soon as you're done feeding the goats, have some breakfast, and then we'll head to the fair."

He didn't say anything about Curtis. "Jason, is my brother going along too?"

"Of course he is. We're not going to leave him here alone in the house."

Yay. I get to spend the day doing fun stuff with Curtis. He won't be so grumpy or mean to me if we are doing fun stuff together. Sometimes, he lets me play army men with him and other times he doesn't. Sometimes he'll throw rocks with me, other times, he won't even answer me if I knock on his door. You never know what kind of mood he'll be in on any given day and it seems to be getting worse, not better.

When I return to the house, Curtis is dressed and eating breakfast. "Anna, did you know that we're going to the fair? We're going to this place where you can ride rides and play games." My brother has a smile on his face. I haven't seen him act happy in a long time.

"Yeah, I'm super excited. Curtis, do you wanna go on a ride with me? Maybe we could sit on the Ferris wheel or a merry-go-round or something together. That would be sooo cool."

"Definitely, I wanna do that." Curtis smiles. Today could be a good day. He seems happy.

Jessica comes into the kitchen. "The town fair is something that everybody looks forward to around here. It's like the last hurrah before all the kids go back to school."

"Back to school?" Curtis and I say it at the same time.

"When do we go back?"

"Two weeks. I already got you and your brother registered, so you're all set to go. You'll be in fifth grade, and Curtis is in fourth. There are visiting hours next week at school so you can have a tour and meet your teachers if you like."

81

"No thank you, I don't want to go see it." It isn't hard for me to answer that question.

"Me either," Curtis blurts out and puts his head down and folds his arms over his chest. Oh no, I see the vein in his forehead pop out and that's not a good sign.

"How are you going to finish eating with your arms crossed? Let's hurry and eat so we can leave." Jess giggles while tickling the top of his head.

I rub my ears. My brother doesn't whisper anymore when he talks. It always seems like he's yelling at the top of his lungs and my eardrums tingle after he does it.

I don't want to think about school,. so, I'm not going to ask any more questions. I don't want it to ruin my day.

***

I look at all the rides.

"Ten balls for a dollar. Stand right up and try your luck." A teenager waves us over to the toss-a-ball-into-a-cup game.

Curtis goes first. It doesn't go in.

"Wow, Curtis. You almost did it." I hand him another small, yellow ball.

"Young man, if you get that ball to stay in the cup, you can pick any stuffed animal you like."

My brother hates stuffed animals and has never had one, so I'm sure he'll give it to me if he wins. That would be nice. That would show me that my brother still loves me, because he knows how much I adore them.

Curtis points to a giant, fluffy bear hanging from the tent roof. "I can do this, Anna. I'm gonna win that big bear right there."

A kid next to him laughs. "*Sure* you will."

If it wasn't for Jessica and Jason standing right here, Curtis would've turned around and punched that kid right in the face. He's so angry anymore and he is always looking to fight with someone at home, so it wouldn't take much for him to fight a stranger right now. But, instead, he throws the ball.

It lands smack in the middle of the cup.

Ha! Curtis showed that jerk.

The kid running the game high-fives Curtis. "Way to go, dude. We have a winner!"

"I want that one." He points to the biggest one they have. "That one."

Curtis tucks the bear under his arm and hangs on to it like I did with my doll when Sue gave it to me for Christmas. My heart sinks. I was wrong. My brother didn't offer me the bear. Maybe he needs it for himself right now like I needed my doll.

After what felt like just a few hours, Jessica and Jason announce that we must go because it's getting late. I didn't realize it was dark because all the lights are lit up around the fair, making it look like daylight. We've been here all day, riding rides and playing games. Curtis still has the bear under his arm like he did after winning it. The bear rode every ride with us, tucked next to Curtis. I stare longingly at the merry-go-round, wishing we could ride it one more time. The horse I sat on earlier reminded me of Thunder. It was nice to pretend we were together again.

"As soon as we get in the house, we have to hit the hay," Jason says after we get into the car and leave the fun behind.

I look over at my brother on the ride home. He's sleeping and stays that way all the way to the house.

Jason turns off the engine and looks over his shoulder at us in the back seat. "Jessica, you take Anna in and I'll carry Curtis. He's sound asleep."

"Sounds good, honey. Did you see him sleeping on that bear? I *so* want to help him. I truly do."

Jason puts his hand on her shoulder. "I know you do, sweety. It may take some time." Jason rubs her cheek and Jessica winks at him. There it is again. That's their code to stop talking when we're around. And… I was right. They stopped talking about Curtis. I'm so tired I jump into bed without brushing my teeth.

Goodnight, Jesus. Thank you for having this family take me to the fair. I had fun riding the rides you made. I would talk to you longer tonight, but I'm really tired, and I'm yawning cause I'm gonna fall as…

My brother's shrieking jars me awake. "Get away from me!" Curtis screams. "Leave me alone! I don't want to be here! I want to go home!"

I fly out of bed and run to his room. Again.

Chapter 11
Throwing Rocks

"Stop it! Leave my brother alone!" I run into the bedroom and jump on Jason's back, who's holding Curtis to the ground. What the heck is he doing? Is he trying to wrestle him? That won't happen. No way.

"Anna, please stop. Honey, I'm not hurting your brother. I'm helping him." I lose my grip on Jason's neck as he moves his body to the right and then the left.

*No, this can**not** be happening, not again. I thought these people were going to be nice. I didn't think they would hurt us.*

Jess pulls me off Jason's back. "Honey, look at the window." Her soft voice calms me down as she walks backward, holding me off the floor with her arms around me. Eventually, she sits on the bed with me on her lap. The comforter protects my skin from my fingernails cutting into it.

Jess's breath tickles my ear. We're here to assist Curtis, not harm him.

A cool wind comes out of nowhere and caresses my face. I turn my head to find the source. The bedroom curtains flutter from the strong breeze passing through his shattered window.

"Get off me! I hate you! I want to leave!" My brother is crying and shouting so loud he sounds like he's choking. "I can't breathe!"

"He can't breathe. Let him up." I plead with Jason. My brother is in trouble, which makes my body want to fight. It's not okay for big people to damage us small people, and no matter how much I like Jason or Jess, I will not stand here and let them hurt him.

"Jason, let him up but make sure he doesn't go towards the opening," Jess says.

Jason's bear hug stays in place as Curtis sits up. "Buddy, I am going to let you up, but I will not let you go. We can't have you throwing things out the bedroom window or let you jump out."

Curtis screams and spit flies out of his mouth. "You're a liar! I didn't try to jump out of the window. Let me go!"

"I saw your body leaning out of the broken window. I was worried about you. I'm trying to keep you safe."

"I wasn't going to jump. I was looking at the stuff I threw outside. If you don't want me here, call my last mom. She'll take me back. I don't want to be here anymore."

"Buddy, we've been going at this for the past two months now. I wish I could take you back to your last foster mother, but the rules of foster care do not allow us to do that."

Curtis's red and blotchy face looks like it stings. Purple veins pop out everywhere. "No, you don't. You don't want me to be happy. You hate me." His punch lands on Jason's arm. Our foster father doesn't react at all.

"It's okay. It's okay. I get you're mad. I would be too. I want you to be happy. That's all I want for you."

Staying quiet is difficult for me, and even harder when my brother hurts. "Curtis, stop. Please stop. I don't want you to go back to Sue. I want you to be here with me. Please stop."

Going back to Sue is not an option, and he has to accept it. I can't do foster care without him. It's just him and me in this big world, and I would die without him. But, all he cares about is Sue. Why? I need my brother. Tears of frustration and fear flood my eyes. Damn it. Why am I not more important to him than that nasty woman, Sue?

"Jessica, why don't you take Anna out of here? I can tell by her face she's upset."

"I agree, honey. Anna, I'm sure this is hard to see. But I think it'd be better for Curtis if he doesn't feel like we are all around him watching."

She takes my hand as we stand up. "No, I want to stay here with my brother." I yank my hand back.

Curtis whips his head and looks at me. His blue eyes look black. His nostrils flare. "Get the hell outta my room." His words pierce my ears. I didn't know words could cut like a knife. But—I do now.

The smell of sweaty skin fills my brother's room. He and Jason are both soaked. I lock eyes with the stranger who sits on the floor with Jason.

With clenched teeth, Curtis yells. "Get out of my room, or you are going to regret it." He takes a breath. "Get out!" His horrible scream scares me, and I turn and run out of the room.

The hallway wall, covered in vine wallpaper, stops my fall. My hands fill with tears as if I was holding them together to collect water. I hide my face from Jess. She pets my hair like I'm a cat.

"I'm sorry, Anna. It's not okay for you to be the target of his anger. It's not okay that he takes it out on you. He's hurting, and that's why he's lashing out at you like he is."

I want to scream with all the muscles in my body. *Shut up! Foster care did this to Curtis. Mrs. Alex did this to Curtis. I... I... did this to Curtis. It's not his fault.*

"How about we go get something to drink or eat? Jason is trying to help Curtis. We would never hurt either of you. I promise you that."

Promise? How can Jess promise me anything? Everyone breaks such promises in my life... except for Curtis.

I give up. There's nothing I can do anyway. With each step to get downstairs, my brother's cries burn into my heart. Still, I take each step downward. Jessica guides me to the kitchen and pulls out two bowls, a box of cereal, and milk.

"I'm not hungry or thirsty and would rather go outside. Is that okay?" I need to get away from her because I want to be alone.

She wraps her arms around me. "Honey, I get it. I'm here if you need me."

Thank you. Her hug presses my cheek against—her boobs. I feel their softness. I pull away fast.

"I thought maybe you needed a hug. I didn't mean to make you uncomfortable. I care about you. I'll check on you in a few minutes."

"Can I go outside now?"

"Sure you can."

I use my pain as fuel, just like a car. I don't know if I've ever run this fast before. Within seconds, I'm in the barn with my friends. I throw the pen door open, slamming it behind me. The hay stabs my ear as I throw myself into Black Betty's hay pile. "Why is Curtis so different here?" I try to hold back the tears, but I can't. I sob, and every part of my body shakes and I curl up into myself.

"Curtis, please stop. Why can't we be like kids with a mom and dad and not foster parents? Why does Jesus make us live this way? Why wouldn't he want us to have a mom and dad?"

I cry and cry and cry until Black Betty plops down next to me. "Hey you. Thank you for taking care of me when I'm sad." I hug her, but my arms don't go around her belly since she's not a baby anymore. "I love you, Black Betty." I close my eyes.

***

I swipe my nose. I swipe again. "What the heck?" My eyes open to see Curtis holding a piece of straw he's dragging across my face.

"Wake up, Anna. Wake up."

He's laughing as hard as he was crying earlier. "Look at you. I bet you thought it was a bug."

I'm mad. "Stop it." I hit the straw off my face. "Knock it off, Curtis."

"Ha. Ha. Ha." He laughs louder and louder.

"Knock it off." I jump up. "Stop it. It's annoying." I quit yelling at him when it hits me that my brother is laughing. I join in.

The goats run out in the pasture as we laugh.

"Come on, Anna, let's go throw rocks."

"All right. Let's do it, but not for long because I didn't eat breakfast yet and I'm hungry."

Curtis runs ahead of me. "See? I have everything all ready. We each get ten. We're gonna throw them at the same time to see which one goes the farthest." His foot points to my stack of rocks.

"Okay, I see my pile and I'm ready, but why should I bother? You're only going to kick my butt, anyway."

"I know I will." He jumps up and down with a rock in his hand.

My brother is seriously weird sometimes because he can stand here all day and throw rocks if our foster parents would let him, but I play his

87

game, anyway. He really likes to beat me. This is about the only thing he's ever beat me in, every time.

"Get ready." Curtis poses with the rock in his hand in the air.

I have my stone in my hand.

"On your mark, get set, and... go!"

Our stones fly, then crash into the water, only to come out and back in again, over and over.

"Darn it. Mine dies at three skips." Curtis's is still going.

Curtis sings and dances after his rock skips seven times. "You suck. I'm so much better at this than you. Neener neener. You can't beat me."

I swear my brother only likes me to play this game so he can beat me. We do the same routine multiple times until we're finally down to our last two rocks. He yells out the exact instructions as he did eight times before.

"On your mark, get set, and... go."

Both stones fly. One... two... five... and six.

Curtis's stone sinks.

Mine... doesn't. "Holy crap! I beat you. I *finally* beat you. Your rock only went six times." I jump around in circles. "I can't believe I beat you—".

My face smacks into the sand on the beach. Curtis is pounding the back of my head. I can't move for a second because I don't know what's happening. Then... I feel his fist slam into the back of my head. Curtis is beating me. Every part of my body heats like a stove. I wrap my arm around my back and pull him off of me until he is lying under me.

Smack. His punch sends my face to the side. I roll quickly and get up. With lightning speed, so does Curtis. He lunges at me. With all my anger, I shove him to the ground. He falls on his butt. I look down at him with my fist in front of my face as he screams.

"I hate you. I hate you! You had to beat me at this, too. It's not enough that you're stronger than me, can run faster, and play baseball better, too. You can't just let me be better at something than you." Curtis jumps up and runs in my direction.

I will not fight my brother anymore. I won't. I know he's hurting, and it's not his fault. It doesn't matter what I want, though. He jumps on me, and we both fall down at the same time. My back slams into the sandy beach. He lands a few more punches on my face before I put my hands up to protect myself.

Someone lifts Curtis into the air.

"Damn it, Curtis. That hurt." Jason puts his hand up in front of his face to protect himself. "Curtis! Just stop it."

He keeps swinging at Jason. These nice people are going to make us move if Curtis doesn't stop being so mad all the time. I like it here. Curtis and I no longer bring up foster care, as it makes him furious.

No one will get this except for Curtis. What I understand regarding foster care is that every time I made a foster parent mad, we got moved. I made Mother mad in my first foster home by telling Daddy what Derek did to me. They moved us the next day. Sue got mad at me when I told her I didn't want to do girl time anymore, and they moved us that same week. I know Mrs. Alex told us it was because of a house fire. I think she lied to us. I know Sue was mad at me. I remember. These people have to be getting mad by now. Curtis throws fits every day.

Everything around me spins and goes gray. I don't get it. I don't know what is happening. I hear Jess scream. "Curt—"

I wake up to Jess, lightly tapping my face.

"Anna? Anna? Can you hear me? Anna?"

I blink. "What happened?"

"I think you hyperventilated and passed out."

There she goes again, using big words. "I what?"

"You passed out, but you'll be okay."

"Where's Curtis?" I try to sit up.

"Easy, move slowly. Jason is with Curtis now."

I ignore her and sit up fast. "I want to see my brother." There he is, on a bench with Jason… "Curtis, I didn't mean to beat you."

My brother whips his head around, and his beady, black eyes look scary, scrunched together. "Don't talk to me. I don't want to talk to you."

"I'm sorry. I didn't mean it. I didn't do it on purpose."

"Shut up, Anna."

Curtis turns back around and I'm *all* alone. All by myself. No one. No Daddy, no friends from church school, and, now, no Curtis.

Doesn't anyone want me?

Why not?

"Honey, let's walk inside and leave Jason to talk to Curtis." She helps me stand up, and we walk to the house. He aids me with her arm around my waist.

My face throbs. I touch my cheek—there's a big bump there.

"Be careful. Your face is pretty banged up. It's not okay for your brother to hit you like that."

"He didn't mean it."

"Has your brother always acted this way toward you?"

Jess and her questions again. "What do you mean?" I hold my breath. "My brother has never hit me before we lived here. Ever."

She shuts the door, and we stop in the foyer. She stares at me with her hands on her hips and her head falls close to one shoulder. "That's a little hard for me to grasp. He's targeted you many times since you've lived with us. This is not something that just starts one day."

After living with her for a few months, I know Jess well enough to know she doesn't believe me when her head tilts to the side. I have to convince her that my brother is not a monster.

"He never hit me before we came here," I yell as I get mad at her.

"Honey, I can see you are getting angry with me. You don't have to protect your brother by covering for him anymore. We're here to help you and can find a program to help Curtis."

My heart rate picks up speed. What is she talking about? What program? Why is she using words I don't know right now? She knows I'm getting mad.

I scream at her. *Stop it*! Believe me. I feel like I'm hollering into a canyon, but I'm not. It's in my head. "I was always the one fighting. I was the one protecting him. He was always quiet. He's just mad because he wants to go back to our old foster mother, that's all. It's my fault we had to leave the last house."

I break free from Jessica and run upstairs. I said too much. I jump onto my bed and grab my doll to cry all over her.

Like many times before, I'm tired from crying so much...

The knock on my door...

My heart speeds up, and the lump returns to my throat.

Curtis?

Chapter 12
Brother & Sister

"Anna? It's me, Jess. Can I come in?" My heart falls to the floor. I wanted it to be Curtis.

I want to tell her no, but I don't want to be mean because she's nice. So, I squeeze my doll harder. "Yeah."

Jessica comes in with a sandwich on a plate. "Honey, I brought you something to eat because you haven't eaten yet today, which may be why you passed out as well. I'll put it here for when you're ready." She puts it on my dresser. "Can I sit down?"

No, you can't. I want you to leave me alone. I want you to be a great doctor and make my brother better. That's what I *want* to tell her, but, instead, I say, "Sure."

"I want to talk about you and Curtis." She walks over to me and sits on my bed. "Honey, it's not good for you that your brother calls you names, threatens to hurt you, and worse yet, physically beats you up as he did."

She's right, but telling her that will not help my brother. She's not telling me something I don't already know. She has no clue that at nighttime, when I'm trying to fall asleep, all my mind wants to do is think about leaving here because of how much Curtis and I fight.

"I know that."

Have you heard about domestic violence?" she asks.

"Huh?" I don't try to repeat her big words right now because I'm not in the mood. I must've said the wrong thing, because Jessica takes that as an opening to talk with me.

"Domestic violence is when someone you live with has aggressive or abusive behavior toward you or someone else you live with." Everything she says makes no sense to me.

"I don't get it."

"When someone is abusive toward another they live with, that's domestic violence."

This doesn't help me, either. "What does abusive mean?"

"Anna, your caseworker has never talked to you about someone abusing you? Has she ever asked if anyone has hurt you, like I asked you before?"

I shake my head slowly while holding my doll.

"Let me explain. Abuse is when someone hurts you by hitting you, calling you names, making you do sexual things to them, or they do sexual things to you. Do you know what I mean?"

More big words. I have no clue about some of what she is saying. "Sexual? I've never heard that word before," I whisper.

Jessica's hand rests on my shoulder. "Sexual abuse is when someone makes you touch their private parts, or they touch your private parts or any other parts of your body in a way that doesn't feel good. Even kissing can be sexual abuse if someone kisses you on the lips for a long time. If anyone wants to touch your private parts with their hands or private area—no one should ever do this to you as a child. Even as an adult, it should not happen without your permission. Has this ever happened…" Jessica's voice fades.

"Oh."

"If someone did those things to you, it's not your fault. It's theirs. You're a child. Did anyone ever do this to you?" Jess's voice is so soft I can barely hear her.

I bury my head in my doll's hair.

Jess leans closer. "Honey, you can tell me. I can find someone to help you. If something happened, that is."

Find someone to help me? Does that mean I might have to leave again if Jess has to find someone else to help me? If that's what she means, then I'm taking no chances. No way I'm telling Jess now what Derek did in my first foster home—how he sexually abused me because he hurt my girl parts with his finger. And how Sue sexually abused me, too, because she made me suck on her boobies like a baby.

So nope, I'm not telling her anything. I don't want Jess to find anyone else to help me. I don't want to leave my goats, and so far, Jessica and Jason are friendly people and I don't want to leave them either.

So, I lie. "No, nothing's happened to me like that before, and Curtis never beat me up before either." I keep my head down, staring at the comforter on my bed.

"Anna, I think you're in denial."

"What?" I lift my head.

"I think you're not telling me how long this has been happening because you're trying to protect your brother. Have you not seen your face yet?"

I shrug.

"When you do, you'll see that you have a swollen black eye and an enormous bruise on your cheek from your brother's attack." She rubs my arm. "This is domestic violence, and it's not okay. He needs help."

I want to scream at her because she's not *getting* it. Instead, I look directly into her eyes and do not look away. "My brother has never hit me before, and I'm not lying."

"Let me ask you… what would've happened today if Jason hadn't pulled him off of you?"

I shrug again. "I would've gotten up. I'm pretty strong and can care for myself with my brother."

"What happens when Curtis gets older and bigger and hits you?"

I pause to think. "Well, then, I'd hit him back," I smirk.

"Fighting is not the best way to handle things. My job as your foster parent is to create a safe place for you to live in. Unfortunately, I fear I'm failing."

I don't get it or want to. I just want my brother and my goats. "I'm not worried about my brother. Once he gets used to living here, he'll get better and stop fighting me."

Jessica doesn't argue, but, instead, makes a noise with her mouth. "Mmmm. Have you ever seen any other adult hit or hurt another in the foster homes you've lived in?"

This is the first easy question Jessica has asked me so far. "Nope. Daddy and Mother never got into fights in our first foster home, and Sue and Allen never had a fight in front of us, either."

"I'm glad to hear that," she says with a smile, kisses the top of my head, and then leaves.

I know Jess is smart because she's a doctor, but she's crazy. She doesn't know what she's talking about. Curtis is not like Derek and Sue, and he's not doing domestic violence on me like they did. They wanted to hurt me... Curtis doesn't.

***

"Anna?"

Curtis! Please be Curtis this time and not Jess coming back to talk some more. My heart races with excitement, hoping it's my brother.

I fling my door open. Curtis stands there with tears streaming down his face like the creek water at our first foster home. I hug him quickly.

He breaks the hug. "Okay. Okay. Enough already."

"Curtis, I'm so sorry. It was just luck that I beat you."

"I don't think so, Anna. You've gotten close a couple times. You threw a good rock."

My brother seems so much better now. "Come into my room."

Curtis sits on my bed. "I'm sorry I hurt your face. I didn't mean to do that. I was so mad that you beat me..."

"Curtis, I'm sorr—"

"Let me talk, please." He takes a deep breath. "You've beaten me at everything from the time we were little. You beat me at racing up the road to the sluice fort. You played better football than me. Even at baseball, you were better than me—and all the guys on the team knew. You could even spit further and climb a tree faster than me. Finally, I could beat you at something—until today." Curtis wipes his eyes. "Why do you have to be so good at everything? Why can't I be strong like you?"

94

"You *are* strong, Curtis. Look at everything you can do."

The vein in his neck pops out.

I hold my breath.

"Anna." Curtis takes a bunch of small breaths. "Anna. I'm so sorry. I don't want to hurt you."

"I know you don't, just like I don't want to hurt you. But, Curtis, why are you so mad? I know you miss Sue, but you have to let her go, just like I let Daddy go. Go back and see her when you get bigger. That's what I'm going to do with Daddy. We have no choice now. But when we get big, watch out world, here comes Curtis and Anna Snow." I giggle.

"You got that right, sis. I'm going to be the best fisher ever and you are going to be the best..." He pauses.

I'm still stuck on the fact that he called me sis. That's never happened before. I shrug because I don't want to get too excited about it. He is so moody and he may never say it again.

"I, um… am going to be the best… um." I giggle. "I guess I never thought about it."

"I know. I know. You are going to be the best talker ever because that is what you want to do all the time. You never stop talking." Curtis knows me. I love to talk. I giggle with him.

"I agree. That's it. I'm going to be the best talker ever and tell everyone about all the stupid rules with foster care."

I hold up my hand. *Smack.*

"Ouch."

We both shake our hands in the air—our high-five stings.

"I'm never leaving you, Curtis, never. No matter how much you punch me." We both laugh. "Maybe I shouldn't have taught you to fight, but I didn't know you'd use it on me someday." We laugh some more. "You want to go get your bear and bring it in my room with me and my doll and I'll read us a book?"

"Sure." He runs to his room and comes back with Teddy, as he calls him, tucked under his arm.

My doll and I sit close to Curtis and Teddy.

"This is about Dr. Smith's journey to the unknown—"

"Kids, time for dinner. It's homemade mac-and-cheese with burgers."

Curtis jumps out of bed, leaving Teddy on my pillow. Food always makes him move like lightning. "Race you downstairs." He wiggles his eyebrows. "Ready, set, and… go!"

We race to the bottom of the stairs. Though he is faster than me tonight, I can't say I would have beaten him even if I tried because I wouldn't want to make him mad.

"Well, look at you two. You seem in a better mood, Curtis," Jess sounds cheerful.

My brother doesn't speak to Jess like he does to Jason, I guess because he doesn't have anything to say to her. I don't know why he always acts mad at her. It's not her fault we had to leave Sue's. Maybe he's mad at all girls because Sue was a girl, and that's why he doesn't talk much to Jess. That's how I am with Daddy. No one will ever take his place. I didn't get close to Allen in our last foster home because I don't want to get close to another man other than Daddy. But, Jason reminds me so much of Daddy in how he looks and acts, I couldn't help but warm up to him.

"Let's get the table set. Supper is ready."

"How's the mac-and-cheese?" Jason asks after we start eating.

Maybe if I speak for both of us, Jess will see that my little brother is not a monster. "Jess, it's fantastic. Curtis and I both love your mac-and-cheese."

"We would like to talk with you both about something," Jess says, but then stops.

I look up, and Jess's eyes are huge.

What is it?" I mumble.

"Jason and I have decided…"

I'm confused. Jess looks like she has tears in her eyes as she tries to tell us something.

"Why are you crying?" I don't mean to be nosy, but I can't help it.

"Let Jess finish, as she has a surprise for you both. She's just happy about your surprise tonight," Jason says quietly as his eyes stay focused on our foster mother.

Chapter 13
Sand Angels

Jess's voice cracks and her eyes look red. "We've decided that tonight you both can stay up together as long as you like."

Curtis claps. "This is so cool."

I don't say a word, my hands shaking in my lap. Instead, I watch Jess's puffy eyes and her head that falls so her chin is on her chest. I've never seen her this way the entire time we've lived here.

Jess's chair hits the table as she gets up and leaves the room with her hands over her face.

I bite my lip. Something doesn't feel right. Why would Jess be sad about telling us we can stay up all night? I thought surprising kids with something fun makes adults happy.

Jason looks at us. "She's just tired. I'm sure she's going to bed. As she said, the two of you can stay up as late as you want, but here are the rules."

Curtis stops running in place. "*Rules*? Why do we have to have rules?" he asks.

His voice is calm and even. During our time with this family, Curtis seems to only be able to express himself through his loud, angry outbursts, or fits, as I call them. It's nice to hear my brother sound like his old self again. I missed him.

"We have to make sure both of you are safe, and sometimes we have to make decisions that are hard to make, to make sure you both get what you need to be safe."

What's he talking about? We get to stay up as late as we want. Why do we need all these details to do that? My lip hurts. It's been a long time since I bit it. I push my plate away and stand up, close to Curtis.

"The television must be low so it doesn't wake anyone else in the house. I'll be sleeping downstairs in the den if you need anything. Do you understand the rules?"

"Yup, I do," my brother says, whispering.

Jason's eyes get big as he looks at Curtis. "Hey bud. I haven't heard you talk that calmly or quietly since you've been here."

My brother says nothing to him.

"That's how he usually talks. He used to talk like that all the time before we got here." I put my hands on my hips. I've been trying to tell these people this since we arrived.

Curtis still says nothing.

"Is Jess coming back down?" I tilt my head up, narrowing my eyes in confusion.

"I don't think so. It's been a long, emotional day so I'm sure she went to bed."

I'm completely clueless when it comes to understanding what emotional means. "Okay."

"Let's go, Anna. We have all night to do what we want. What do you want to do for—"

Jason clears his throat. "Jess put all kinds of food out for you to eat in the living room. She has popcorn, candy, and some cereal in a bowl for you to snack on." Jason heads out of the room. "I'm heading to bed. And... no leaving this house." He disappears around the corner.

Why does my belly hurt? It feels like it does when I get scared, but I'm not afraid of staying up alone with my brother, so, I rub it a little more before Curtis jumps in front of me.

He grabs my hand and pulls me into the living room. "Popcorn." He throws it at my face.

I open my mouth quickly, catching it.

"One point for you. Your turn."

I toss a piece of popcorn at him. He catches it and the next four. I catch only three.

Curtis twirls around. "I'm the winner! I'm the popcorn-catching champion!"

"Curtis, be quiet. We don't want Jason to make us go to bed." I grab his hand and pull him to the sofa. "Let's see what's on television."

I go to the TV and turn the knob, but nothing we want to watch comes on.

I walk back and lean close to Curtis and whisper, "Wanna try to go outside?"

"Yeah!" His eyes are enormous.

"Okay but follow me and be quiet."

We tiptoe to the door. "Shhh," I say as I turn the handle on the back door. We don't use the front because it's too close to the den.

He nods.

Click. The lock sounds like a huge drum when I turn it.

Thirty seconds later, we're standing on the back porch. I close my eyes—the smell of fresh-cut grass swarms around me.

"Anna, come on." Curtis runs across the yard toward the lake.

I follow. I freeze as my bare feet hit the sand. *Then, suddenly, I'm back to rolling around over the sand fighting with Curtis. "No, I scream. No. Curtis, stop it!"* The beach reminds me of our fight from this morning and of my angry brother.

"Anna, come on."

My brother's voice snaps me out of my thoughts. He's in the water. Oh, he's swimming. What a great idea. The lake water flies up around my legs as I run in with my nightgown on. A huge splash of water hits my face. Giggling. My brother is happy right now. I really think I have my brother back.

"You wanna play?" I send a massive wave of water toward Curtis, slamming into him. He takes both of his hands and pushes an enormous wave towards me. My face hurts from laughing so much. "Curtis, let's jump off the dock, but we have to be quiet."

"You first, Anna."

I bend my knees as I jump so my feet don't hit bottom. *Splash.* "Curtis, make sure you keep your legs bent so you don't hit the bottom."

Splash. "That's so much fun. Let's do it again." He comes out of the water yelling.

"Shush. Be quiet. We don't want them to hear us." I point to the house. I'm having so much fun with you, Curtis. We used to do this all the time."

"I'm sorry, Anna. All I could think about was going back to Sue. But… I don't want to ever leave you. I'm sorry I hurt you." It's too dark to see him, but his hand moves by his eye.

After what seems like most of the night playing in the water, we decide to get out. Curtis falls backward, landing in the sand.

"Let's make sand angels." He laughs. He lays flat and makes his legs and his arms open and closed across the sand.

It seems to work, so I do the same.

We lay on our backs on the sandy beach after our sand angels are made, looking up at the stars.

"Anna?"

"Yeah?"

"Why do you think no one wants us?"

"I don't know."

The crickets sing together as we lay in the dark.

"What's wrong with us? Do we do something that makes people hate us?"

"I don't know." I've been wondering the same thing and have come up with nothing.

"Maybe it's about the big people and not us. Maybe we just end up living with big people who can only take care of kids for so long."

"I really don't know, Curtis."

Curtis takes a big breath and holds it. "I really miss our mom, Sue, and her big hugs. She was good to us."

If only I could tell Curtis that she wasn't good to me. Maybe someday, when he's big, I can tell him all the things Derek and Sue did to me.

Maybe.

"Curtis?"

After a few seconds, he answers. "Yeah?"

"Jess and Jason seem like nice people. Though, they *do* keep reminding us that they are our foster parents. It's clear they don't want to be our mom and dad, but do we really want a mom and dad anyway?"

He responds without hesitation. "Nope. I don't. I had a mom in Sue and I will never have another one."

"That's how I feel about Daddy, so I know what you mean."

He grabs my hand. "It's just you and me. We will never leave each other. Never."

I squeeze his hand harder. "Never, Curtis. I will never leave you."

Mahhhm. Mahhhm. I jump "Holy crap! The goats are out of their pen and on the beach with us." I'm on my feet in no time. "Be careful, we don't want to scare them into the water. I don't know if they can swim. Come on, maybe they'll follow us back to the barn."

My plan works and Curtis and I lead the goats into the barn. I fall on a pile of straw in the barn hallway. "This is one of my favorite smells in the whole, wide world."

"You like the smell of shit?" He cracks up. "It's so cool to swear, Anna. When I'm a grown-up, I'm going to swear all the time."

That makes me giggle. "I bet you will. Curtis, when you grow up, what do you want to do? I mean for real, other than being the best fisher on earth."

"I'm going to drive the biggest monster truck I can find. I'm gonna be cool like Fonzie." A gigantic smile grows on his face.

"Fonzie has black hair, silly, and you have white. You can't look like Fonzie."

"I never said I was gonna *look* like him. I said I am gonna be cool like him." He puts his thumbs in the air. "Aye."

My face hurts because I am laughing so much with my brother.

"Anna, what do you want to be when you grow up? You never answered."

I take a deep breath and think hard. Finally, I know. "I'm going to tell everyone what it's like to be a foster kid. I—"

"You're gonna do what?" Curtis's eyes widen in surprise at what I just said.

"I want to help other foster kids like us. You know, the kids no one wants."

"Maybe you should become a doctor, like Jess."

"Nah. I don't want to give people needles. I just want to help them feel better."

Curtis is quiet. "Maybe we're the only foster kids."

I never thought about that. "If we are them, I will tell everyone our story. What's it like to be like us... foster kids carrying garbage bags everywhere."

Curtis' voice goes deep. "I hate it."

"Me too Curtis. Me too. But I do like living here."

"Yeah, I guess they're nice. We never know when we'll have to start again, when we will have to find a new place to call home. We didn't know the times before, so why even try to like people? What's the point? We are only going to move away from them, anyway."

Another good point by my brother. "If we don't get close to people, who will we have besides each other?"

Curtis sighs. "Who else do we need besides each other?"

"You're right. I don't need anyone but you. No matter how much we move, as long as you are with me, I'll be okay." I hit his hand.

"Me too Anna."

"I'm tired," I say.

"Me too. Should we go inside?"

"Nah, why don't we sleep right here in the barn?"

"Sounds good to me."

We take the next few seconds to cover up with hay. It's warm, but our clothes are still wet.

"Good night, Anna. I love you."

"Good night, Curtis. I love you, too."

For the first time since we got here, my heart feels better because I have my brother back. Nothing is better than this feeling.

Nothing.

***

"Curtis? Anna? Curtis? Anna?"

I'm jerked awake by Jess and Jason screaming our names.

I nudge Curtis. "We have to get in the house fast. I hear Jason and Jes—"

The barn door slams against the wall boards.

"There you two are," Jess says and takes a big breath at the same time. She bends over in the middle of talking to catch her breath.

Jason takes quick, deep breaths like he ran a race. "You two had us worried sick. We could tell you were in the lake last night. We saw your sand angels on the beach, and all we could think was that the two of you had drowned or something crazy."

102

"We need you both to come into the kitchen because we need to talk about something," Jess doesn't look any better than last night before she went to her bedroom. Her eyes are puff, she has no makeup on and she walks around with her chin sitting on her chest. She looks sad. Why?

Curtis runs into the house and I follow. I try to brush straw from my pjs as I run.

"We spent so much time looking for you this morning. We don't have much time." Jess and Jason follow us as they speak.

I scrunch my eyes together. What's Jess talking about? We only have a little time for what?

As we get through the front door, I hear it.

The engine. I know that engine.

Please, Jesus, don't let that be Mrs. Alex's car.

Just then her ugly, green nightmare pulls up the driveway.

Chapter 14
Please

I scream as loud as I can at Curtis. "Curtis... run!"

He and I take off in a fast sprint up the stairs to my bedroom and I slam my bedroom door shut, and then dart for my bed. We don't hear Jason or Jessica behind us coming up the steps.

Curtis speaks so quietly I can barely hear him. "Anna, I have to get my bear out of my room."

Who am I to say no when I'm curled on my bed holding my doll? "You stay here. I'll get it for you."

I tiptoe to my door and put my ear against it, hoping I can hear if anyone is upstairs... but I don't hear anything. Fast like lightning, I run to Curtis' room and grab Teddy off his bed. I slam my door harder than I should've because I don't want them to know where we are. I go to Curtis, who's curled up in my bed.

He grabs my hand with one hand and his bear with the other. "Anna, why are we in your room?"

Oh, right? I didn't tell my brother why to run. He just did it because I told him to. "I saw Mrs. Alex's car."

"You *what*?" My brother's face goes white, and he instantly shakes and his breathing gets faster. "Are you sure? Go look out your window. You can see the driveway from here." My brother points to the window facing the barn.

Quietly, I tiptoe across my pink carpet, and then peek out. Mrs. Alex is putting a garbage bag in her car, and Jessica and Jason are standing beside her, crying. What's in the garbage bag? Oh no. We're being moved again. I run to my dresser and open a drawer.

"Anna, what are you doing?"

"Hold on, I'm checking something." I pull out each drawer, and my clothes have not been touched. They're still folded exactly like Jessica likes to do. If my clothes are in my dresser, then what...?

Curtis cries. "What are you doing? What's going on?"

"Mrs. Alex put a garbage bag in her car, but all of our clothes are still in the dressers."

Curtis' eyebrows rise. "Why is Mrs. Alex taking Jessica and Jason's garbage?"

"Good question. I don't know." I grab my red chair and slide it to the window.

"Anna, come back to the bed."

"Give me a second. I want to sit here and watch them." I make sure the chair is off to the side, so that woman can't see me.

"Anna, come back here." Curtis whispered in a soft, high-pitched voice.

It gets worse, though, because we hear them in the house. I walk to the door so I can hear what they're saying. "Come here so we can hear what they're talking about."

Then, the front door opens and then closes.

Curtis shakes his head and squeezes his bear harder. I know my brother needs me right now, but I have to know what's going on and why Mrs. Alex is here. It's never good when she's around.

"This is not going to be easy on them." Jason's voice travels up the stairs.

"Do you really think this is the best thing?" Jessica asks.

"We do this all the time. It's not always best for siblings to stay..." The voices get louder.

I take off in a sprint and jump on my bed next to Curtis. "I think they're coming up the stairs." We wrap our arms around each other and our toys.

The door opens.

"Hey guys." Jason peeks his head in. "Can you come downstairs so we can talk to you?"

The walls in my bedroom seem as if they're getting closer and closer together, like they might squeeze us. The only color I really see in the room is the small, red chair I moved over in front of the window.

Curtis squeezes me.

"No! I shriek.

Jason's eyes grow wider, and he hangs his head.

"We are not going anywhere near that mean Mrs. Alex and you can't make us!" I let out a loud, desperate yell.

Jason speaks softly. "We're not trying to hurt you; we're trying to help you." His voice cracks and his eyes are all puffy, and his nose is red.

I know that look. It was the look my daddy had on his face when he stood in the middle of the road while Mrs. Alex took me away in her car.

"What's going on? I saw Mrs. Alex put garbage in her car. Why is she taking your garbage?"

Jason freezes. The walls get closer and closer to me. The once sunny morning outside my window, with pretty singing birds, is turning black. All I hear is the caw of the crows.

"Anna, you're older. Can you please help me? I need you to bring your brother downstairs so we can talk with you."

"Nope. I'm not doing it. I told you. We're not going near that mean woman." I scream as loud as I can, and then curl in tighter next to my brother. Our hands are wrapped around one another, and we tangle our legs like two people twisted into a pretzel. In this moment, we are one, burrowing our heads into each other, holding on tighter to each other.

I whisper to my brother, "Whatever you do, don't let go of me."

My heart's pounding in my chest and between that, Curtis' heavy breathing—as well as my own—I can't hear Jason. I sneak a peek.

106

"He's gone, Curtis."

Something's going on, but I don't know what it is. I untangle myself and hop off of my bed, leaving my doll in my place next to Curtis, and then walk to the door again.

The sound is muffled, but I think I hear Jess crying. "Maybe we've changed our mind. I think we can make this work."

"I agree," Jason says, his voice all froggy-sounding. "I don't like this idea at all. You should see them up there, hanging onto each other. I'm not going to be the one to do this. You'll have to call for assistance."

"I'm sure I will." Mrs. Alex's nasty, gross voice is louder than the others. "Can I use your phone, please? Anna is a nightmare in these transitions and difficult to control."

"Anna?" Jessica almost yells my name. "Are you sure you don't mean Curtis?"

"Curtis is quiet and doesn't say much. Anna is the wild one you have to watch out for. She'll kick your kneecaps right out from underneath you."

Mrs. Alex speaks like it's no big deal, telling Jess bad things about me. How can she sound so cold and mean? I hate her. I truly hate her. I *will* kick her kneecaps out if she tries to take me and Curtis from here. I will.

"That's not what we've seen here," Jason says. "Curtis has been the aggressive one."

"Will one of you try one more time to get the kids to come down? If you need to, pull them apart," Mrs. Alex says.

"The hell we are." Jason rarely curses.

"You can't ask us to do that. Nor will we. Get help. We will not be part of this craziness. We just told you we changed our mind and can try it a little longer. You're standing here now, telling us we have no choice."

"Yes, you're correct. He doesn't have a choice. When you told me you found a dead, wet kitten by the lake, he lost that right. Such behavior is too concerning."

Dead kitten?

Lucky?

I run back to my bed. "What did you do to Lucky, Curtis?"

My brother says nothing. He's hurt cats before, but now?

"Did you drown Lucky, Curtis?"

My brother burst into tears. "No. I didn't hurt that kitten at all. I was with you all night last night, remember?"

107

I replayed last night over and over in my mind. When would he have had time? Maybe when I was sleeping? He was never alone. It had to be when I was sleeping.

Come to think of it, I didn't hear Lucky at all last night or this morning.

My face is hot, and I feel like my ears are glowing red. "Curtis…" I grind my teeth together as I lean over him. "You tell me right now. Did you kill Lucky?"

My brother cries harder as his face turns purple, and he hiccups and gags like he's choking. "Anna, I swear. I didn't drown Lucky. Please, Anna." He reaches out his arms for me. "I didn't do it. Please believe me." My brother's lips are turning blue. It looks like he's holding his breath.

I jump on the bed next to him and wrap myself around him to help him calm down. My heart aches in so many ways. "I believe you, Curtis. I believe you."

However, I don't really know if I *can* believe him. But… he didn't lie to me back at the sluice pipe fort at Mother and Daddy's when he *did* kill some kittens there—he'd merely nodded when I'd asked him like he didn't even care. He definitely didn't act this upset then, so I *think* he's telling the truth.

Tears burn my eyes as I think about Lucky being dead. She was a beautiful, black kitty. Why is everything so wrong all the time? My whole life is full of crying and pain.

My door flings open. Jessica's there, crying hard with huge, red eyes and a wet face. "I'm sorry." Her voice cracks as she sniffles. "I'm so, so sorry. I never wanted this to happen. I didn't know what else to do. Please forgive me."

She leaves then, sobbing like a baby.

I hear her speaking to Jason in the hallway in a loud, angry voice. "This is the last time I'll ever do foster care, do you hear me? What they're about to do to those two babies in that room is nothing short of the most disgusting thing I've ever seen in my entire life." Her sobs get louder.

"I'm sorry. I know how much you care for them. I'm sorry, honey." Jason sounds sad, too.

No. No. No, we're leaving. They're going to make us move again and go to another house. My heart pounds hard. I'm gasping for breath and I can feel a lump forming in my throat. I don't want to leave this house. I really like it here. Not again, please, not again.

"Anna, you're scaring me. What's going on?" When my brother looks at me, his eyes seem to take up his entire face.

"I think we're leaving, Curtis. Maybe my clothes are still in the dresser because Jessica doesn't want us to take any of the ones she bought us."

He doesn't do or say anything. He's frozen in a small ball. I don't think he could run right now, even if I told him to. I'm the one who'll fight to make sure we're okay, and maybe today, Mrs. Alex's kneecaps *will* come flying off.

I gag. My body is shaking and I can feel my stomach clenching like it's ready to throw up. I jump off the bed and run to the garbage can in my room, bury my face in some papers, and puke until there's nothing left. Then, I wipe my mouth on a shirt hanging in my closet. Everything inside me is scared.

"Curtis I'm scared. I don't want to move again."

Curtis hasn't moved. I climb back on the bed with him, and we stay in our balled-up position together for as long as possible. That is, until the door flies open and two men in blue cop suits come into the bedroom, moving quickly.

"Hey, kids. We're here to help you, not hurt you, so please work with us." They move closer to the bed. "We don't enjoy having to do this, but we have to."

What is it he has to do? What is it he doesn't like?

Mrs. Alex walks in. "Okay, Curtis, you have to come with me. Anna, you'll be staying here."

"What?" I scream with everything I have in me. "You are *not* taking my brother from me!"

I wrap my arms around Curtis and scream as loud as I can, hoping my voice scares them away like a momma bear scares people away from her cubs. A tornado of tears streams down my face. "Leave my brother and me alone!" I scream at the officer over and over again. I wrap myself tighter around Curtis, and we bury our heads into each other, thinking this'll give us more power to stay together.

"I'm sorry, Curtis, but you have to come with us."

"No," I cry. I can't stop my tears, followed by the deep howl of pain that makes all of my insides hurt. "Please, I beg you! Please don't take my brother! Please don't take him from me! He's all I have in the entire world!"

They pull Curtis away from me.

He screams as he loses his grip on my neck. "Anna! Don't let them take me! Please, Anna! No!"

I throw my arms around my brother's waist. "Please don't take him!" I grab blindly as someone pulls my fingers from his blue shirt.

Then, as they lift Curtis in the air, he reaches for me and howls so loud it's like a wolf howling at the moon. "Don't let them take me, Anna!"

I jump up and I'm about to grab his hands again when someone grabs me and pulls me in another direction. I can't see who has me. I flail my arms like I'm swimming, trying to get to Curtis. It's like everything is moving super slow but too fast at the same time. I can't tell which way is up and which way is down. All I know is pain.

They carry him farther and farther away from me. I grab at the air and my tears fall so hard that I can't see anything anymore. My voice cracks as I try to scream at the men. "Please! Please! Don't take my brother! Pleeeeeease!"

My heart is going to explode out of my chest and I don't care. I can't get air. I'm dying. I kick with everything I have, and so does my brother.

"Get him out of here! I can't hold her much longer! Get him in the car," one officer yells to the other.

"I'll get the car door, and you can put him in the back seat," Mrs. Alex yells over our screams.

I can't get to him. I can't reach him. They're stealing him away from me.

"Cuuuuurtisssss! Cuuuuurtisss!"

"Anna, breathe!"

Is that Jessica? I don't care. I have to get to my brother.

But I can't breathe.

"Get out of my way and put her down! Can't you see she's about to pass out? She's hyperventilating. Put her down," Jessica yells.

Everything in the room is blurry—'til it isn't.

"Open your eyes, Anna.."

Daddy? Jesus? Is that you?

"Anna, open your eyes."

I don't want to open my eyes. I want to stay here with Jesus or Daddy. I don't want to go back to the world.

"Anna, open your eyes."

Oh. That's Jessica's voice.

Chapter 15
Dottie

I open my eyes slightly and the white ceiling comes into focus. Everything else is blurry, even the face hovering over me as someone rubs my cheek.

"We need you to wake up, honey."

Everything comes rushing back to me. "Curtis," I scream as I jump up—and then fall down. I cry out in pain. "I have to save my brother!"

I stand and push Jess out of the way, and I run—right into the wall beside the door because everything's still blurry.

"Jason, grab her! She can't see where she's going," Jess says, frantically.

Well, I can now, so I take off in a full sprint to get outside to Curtis. I hold the railing, but I miss steps and almost fall. It's like my body can't keep up with my legs. It'll be faster if I ride the railing.

So I do.

I hit the floor, running. Nothing's going to stop me. I *have* to find my brother. "Curtis!" I race off the porch—The ugly green car is pulling out of the driveway with my life in the back seat, looking out the rear window. "Curtis!"

I don't think. I just run after the car.

Run faster!

Curtis is staring out the car's back window, screaming and hitting the glass.

Run faster! Catch the car! Run faster!

I can hear my body crying out for rest, begging me to stop. I stumble on the rough asphalt and feel the sharp sting of the fall. I shoot up, the sound of my heart pounding in my ears as I keep running. Keep going. Keep going.

Then a stabbing pain nails me in my side that slows me down. I clench my fists and plead with my legs to keep going. I scream in frustration as I saw the green car's tail lights disappear, my feet pounding the road as I race down the center line.

Someone honks their horn behind me, but I don't care. I keep running. "Currrtisss!"

I sob and gasp for air, holding my arms out in front of me. "Currt… issss! Currt… iss!"

My legs give out and I collapse.

I fold myself into a ball and try to scream my brother's name, but I can't… breathe.

I wrap my arms around my stomach. My breathing is getting faster and faster and everything gets fuzzy again.

"Anna, you're not alone. I'm here with you, but it's not safe to stay here. We need to get off the road. A car is behind you." The soft voice sounds kind. Jason?

I squeeze my eyes shut, and I can feel the warmth of my tears dripping down my face and filling the lake of sadness within me. I'm being moved.

"Anna, open your eyes, sweety."

He stares at me, and I can hear him sniffle as his tears slide down his face. "Honey, I'm so sorry. We didn't want this to happen."

"Cur… rrr… tiss. They took my brother from me. They took… him." I wrap my arms around Jason's neck. My tears get his shirt all wet.

They took my brother.
They took him away from me.
They took my… life.

Here I am, stuck in quicksand, feeling like I'm losing all feeling. But, this time, I'm awake. I see Jason's truck parked sideways in the middle of the road, and there are a bunch of cars and tractor-trailers behind it.

"Hey man. Is everything okay?" Some guy asks as Jason puts me in the front seat. "Do you need us to call an ambulance?"

"No, thank you. That won't be necessary. We just have a sad, little girl on our hands. I'll move my truck in a second." Jason shakes the stranger's hand, who then walks behind the truck and out of sight.

Jason gets behind the wheel. "Hey, I have an errand to run that I think you'll like. Want to come?"

I say nothing. I think of nothing. I do nothing.

Jason must've taken my quietness as a sign I agreed. "Okay, honey." The truck jumps forward as he drives to whatever he has to do. "I think you're going to like this errand. Jess has a surprise for you, and you will like it. Jess…" His voice fades as I get lost in the darkness of being sad.

I don't care about surprises. I don't care about anything except getting my brother back. My eyes fill with tears as I lean against the window away from Jason so he can't see me.

Jesus. Why did you take my brother from me? Did I do something to make you mad? Did I hurt your feelings? Why would you do that? I thought you loved me. I thought you would always be here for me. If that's true, then Jesus… why did you hurt me?

The tears fall quietly down my cheeks, into my mouth. *I want my brother. Please, Jesus, give him back to me.* I don't want to be all alone.

I *am* all alone now—with no one.

Curtis has to be afraid. Who's going to talk to him? Who's going to stick up for him? Who's going to love him?

Wait—who's going to love *me* now?

My heart is torn apart as if a wild animal is shredding it. I quietly sob some more and try to catch my breath without Jason noticing. It doesn't take long to get where we are going. The truck comes to a stop.

"We're here." Jason parks.

I wipe my eyes with my bare arm. Then, I look down at my legs. I'm still in my pajamas from last night.

113

"Um, Jason? I'm, um, still in my pajamas."

"That's okay, honey, your pajamas are long and this is my cousin's farm, so we're family. Come on. I have something to show you."

When we arrive, Jason sets me on the ground, barefoot and all.

He takes my hand as we walk to the barn. "Just watch your step. My cousin has a bunch of animals in the barn. I thought this could help you feel better."

If I could find happiness right now in a building, I'd make the barn at our house my home, surrounded by its warm, poopy hay smell. Why does he think a barn is going to make any of this okay, though?

"They have a horse."

I felt a quick but gentle squeeze on my shoulder as Jason's hand brushes against me.

"I hope this may help a little. They have quite a selection, in fact. Again, watch your step. You don't want to step in anything with those bare feet."

The barn door swings open, and four horses stick their heads out of their stalls. I walk ahead of Jason and stop at the first horse. She's tan with a white stripe going down her nose. "Aren't you beautiful?" I try to pet her, but she whips her head away from me. "That's okay. I don't like people touching me either."

I walk to the second stall with a black-and-white dotted horse. "I've never seen this color before."

"This is their champion, Mister Samuel Price Storm. He's a Knabstrupper, which is a very rare breed of horse. My cousin doesn't do anything with this horse except stud him out."

As I walk by the third stall, the horse tries to eat my pajamas like an apple. Thunder. This big, ole horse reminds me of my best friend, Thunder, from my last foster home. He's all black, with a small white spot between his eyes. He even has bigger feet, like Thunder did.

I whimper with tears still escaping my eyes and finding a pathway down my cheek. "You remind me of my old, best friend. You're beautiful." I pet his nose. If only Thunder was here. I would jump on him like I did my old foster home and take off running again. But this time, I wouldn't stop. I bet I could've caught up with Mrs. Alex's car if I'd been riding Thunder.

Curtis? Curtis.

Jason reappears with a wheelbarrow. I know that means he plans to pick up shit. It hits me again—Curtis. He said he was going to grow up and swear a lot just because he can. He laughed at me when I told him I liked the smell of the barn and he said it's because I like the smell of shit.

Without warning, all my pain comes out. I sob loudly and gag.

"Anna." Jason comes running over and leaves his wheelbarrow behind. "Come sit with me. Let's talk for a moment." Jason puts his arm around me then we sit on the hay bale. "It's dawned on me that no one has told you yet why things happened the way they did. Do you want me to tell you?"

What kind of stupid question is that? Of course, I want to know why they stole my brother from me. This is the first dumb thing I've heard Jason say. I cross my arms and nod. I keep my mouth shut; my face so hot it feels like I'm about to burst like a volcano.

"We called Mrs. Alex because we were worried about your brother and his anger. I wanted her to help us with him and maybe find a program that would help with anger management or a counselor."

I sit glued to the hay bale. I want to scream, but nothing comes out when I open my mouth. They shouldn't have called Mrs. Alex because I *told* them that Curtis wasn't always like that.

Jason keeps talking, his voice rising and falling with every sentence. "Mrs. Alex said that she was concerned about your brother killing cats. I guess she got reports from an old foster home that the neighbors found their cats dead."

"How do you know it was my brother? It could've been a wolf or something," I say, snapping.

"Yes, you're right. She reported that there was no clear sign of injury so there's no proof your brother did it, but then we found Lucky. With Curtis being so violent with you, and then finding Lucky, Mrs. Alex thinks he needs to go to a home for boys."

I have to ask questions so I can run away and go find him as soon as I can. "A home for boys?"

"Yes," he says, his voice echoing in the barn. "A group home where lots of boys all live together."

That's not going to be good for my brother. Other boys are mean to him and pick on him all the time about how small he is. Though I *can* say this: my brother can throw a good punch now.

"How far away is this place? Is it in the same town we live in now? Can I walk to it? Can I take a bus to it?" My questions come out so fast I don't give Jason a chance to answer any of them.

"Easy, easy. Sadly, honey," Jason puts his arm around my shoulders again, "it's hours from here. So, the answer is no to all of your questions. It's not someplace you can walk to or take a bus to. This home will help Curtis feel better, and maybe he'll stop being mean to animals." Jason puts his head down and whispers. "Jess and I didn't want this for you two. We're really sorry, Anna." Jason swipes away the tears from his cheeks.

I say nothing. What am I supposed to say? I don't want to talk. I want to scream as loud as I can at all the big people who hurt me. It's because of them that my brother is no longer here. I can tell that Jason is watching me, even without looking directly at him. I don't move.

"I guess I better get the chores done. If you need me, come find me. Jason rises to his feet and takes a few steps away but pauses. His finger moves in the direction of the horse that looks like Thunder. "That giant workhorse really seems to like you."

All the air rushes out of my lungs as my head droops down to my chest. I just want my brother back. My sadness is causing my brain to pound. This has to be a nightmare, and I'm sure I'll wake up soon and everything will be as it was before. Foster care is my real nightmare, though, and… that is my normal now. Maybe it always has been.

I head over to the giant black horse, who lowers his head so I can pet him. "Hey, gorgeous, I wish I could jump on your back and have you take me away from here forever. Or take me to find my brother." I lean against the pen door and slide down until I'm sitting on the hard, barn floor.

An itty-bitty, white kitten with a black spot on its face comes walking toward me. I don't move because I don't want to scare it away. The white kitty rubs up against my leg.

"You're just a baby. Where's your Mama?" I hadn't noticed that Jason was in the stall beside me.

"Sadly, it doesn't have a mama. It's a stray. It just got dropped off yesterday. I gave it some milk this morning and it loved that. So, it's old enough to eat on its own." Jason scrapes up a pile of poop in the hallway. "Darn people drop off kittens at barns. There were two other kittens with that one," he points to the baby, who's in my lap now. "I haven't seen them since yesterday, so, I guess something must've gotten to them."

"Hello, Dottie. I know what it's like for your brother or sister to be taken from you. I bet you're sad like me." I rub her back and tail. "We're the same right now. We have nobody in this entire world." I'm afraid. I'm all alone now.

116

I close my eyes and lay on the cold cement floor with hay sprinkled over it. It doesn't matter to me how uncomfortable or dirty it is. Nothing can be worse than what happened to me today. It's like my brother died. I know they won't let me call him. I know it.

I curl up on the barn floor with Dottie wrapped tight by my belly.

"Anna, honey, it's time to go." Jason nudges me, his voice soft, like I'm in a dream.

Please wake up, Anna. This is all a bad dream. Wake up and you will see Curtis by the lake, throwing rocks.

My eyes pop open, only to realize the dream is my real-life nightmare. Curtis is gone and I'm alone.

"Anna, come on. We have to go. I'm sure Jess has dinner waiting for us."

I hug the kitten. "I don't want to leave this kitty alone. Can I, um…" I take a deep breath. "Can I, um, take Dottie home with me? She's all by herself, just like me. I promise I'll take care of her. I'll even keep her out in the barn since Jess doesn't want animals in the house. Please?"

Jason stands straight up and says nothing at first.

Then, he does.

Jason looks down at Dottie and me. "Okay, as long as you keep the kitten in the barn." He winks. "Now, come on. We have to get going, and bring the furball with you. We wouldn't want it to be alone." Jason's face scrunches up. "I'm sorry about today. I'm sad too and miss your brother, but I'm sure nothing compared to how you feel right now, Anna. Maybe the kitty will give you some company."

He keeps saying the same things over and over, but what does it matter? It's all meaningless. I squeeze Dottie carefully as Jason lifts me into his truck.

Chapter 16
Just Another Goodbye

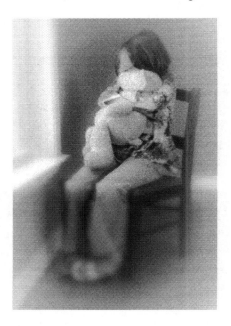

The ride back to the house is quiet, or rather, I block out any conversation Jason tries to have with me. All I want is to go to bed with Dottie.

"We're home." Jason glances at me.

"I'm taking Dottie to the barn. I'll be in later." I mumble my words as I walk away from him.

My feet only take a few steps before I'm stopped in my tracks. My brother's bear, Teddy, is lying in the middle of the driveway. "Jason! My brother's bear. Curtis dropped his bear!"

I pick it up. "Curtis is gonna need this bear to be okay."

"Honey, I'm sure Curtis will be fine without his bear, but, if you want, we can call the caseworker and ask her to come get it and take it to your brother."

I nod. Can she take to me to visit my brother? Jason turns my way, and his eyes are blank, as if the color has been removed from them.

"Okay, I'll tell Jess. I'll help you carry one of them to the barn. It looks like your little hands are full."

I shake my head.

"Do you want me to come to the barn with you? Maybe get the kitty some milk out of the bulk tank? I have to milk the cows, anyway.

I shake my head. I'm not in the mood to hear his voice. I don't need anything from him.

"Okay. I won't bother you. I'll be in the back of the barn milking if you need anything."

I look at him and say nothing. I carry the bear and Dottie to the barn so I can make a new home for her. The faster I walk, the faster my tears fall to the driveway. I'll never stop crying for my brother.

Once I'm in the barn, I put the bear on the ground next to the pen door because Dottie is squirming, so I need both of my hands now. I get her a small bowl of fresh milk out of the tank and carry her and the milk to Black Betty's pen.

After I see that Dottie is drinking the milk, I push a bunch of hay together to make a bed for her. "This should keep you warm, Dottie Dot."

Not only is this a good spot for Dottie to sleep, but me, too. I take Teddy and use him as a pillow while I curl up in a ball.

"Anna? I brought you a sandwich." Jess's shoes crunch on the hay sprinkles as she walks into the barn. "Anna? Are you in here?"

"Yes."

The pen door opens. Jess's eyes are still puffy. "I hear you brought home a kitty. Maybe it'll help you during this rough time. I'm really sorry, honey." She takes a deep breath. "I didn't want this to happen. Please know that we disagreed with it." Jess sniffles and wipes her nose. "Can I sit with you for a second?"

I nod. The thought of trying to talk to her makes my throat tighten. She sounds sad in her voice, but I can't help but put the blame on them for Mrs. Alex taking Curtis from me.

She picks up Teddy so she can sit down, but I rip the bear from her hands. "That's my brother's bear. He must've dropped it when that mean Mrs. Alex and whoever was helping her shoved my brother in the car."

"I'm sorry Anna. Maybe we can call Mrs. Alex today to come get the bear and take it to him. Would you like that?"

"Jason already said he was going to tell you about that," I say, snapping.

Jess tries to smile. "He'll probably tell me about it once he's done milking the cows." She puts the sandwich next to me.

Dottie walks over and sniffs it. The kitten is more interested in eating than I am.

Jess pauses for a moment before speaking again. "I'm sorry. I know this is not easy for you right now, but Jason and I are happy that you will continue living with us." She puts her hand on my leg. Her touch feels like a nail is being hammered right through it. They want me but not my brother? Is that what they did?

I pull back and land a punch in the middle of Jess's face. Her nose bleeds, and she cries out as teeth fall out of her pretty smile and into her hand.

Dottie's meow brings me back and out of my pretend mind. Jess's hand falls away as I move my leg.

"Anna?" Jess is trying to be helpful, but I wish she'd back off and leave me alone. She keeps talking.

"Oh. I'd be mad at us, too, if I were you. But we really were just trying to help your brother."

How does Jess think putting him in a car, going who-knows-where, to a group home full of boys who can be mean to him will *help* him? Even worse, I'm not there to help him. I feel my skin getting warmer and warmer, like an oven heating up.

Jess doesn't realize what's happening since she's still talking. "Do you want to come in with me and watch a movie together?"

They ripped my brother out of my arms this morning, and she wants me to watch a movie with her. I tighten my hands into a fist. My nails cut into my skin. I shake my head.

"No, I don't want to." Why would Jess think I'd want to sit and watch a movie? Don't these big people realize they have just taken away the only thing that I ever cared about? I'm ten years old and I have nobody. I want to yell at her to stop bothering me.

"Okay. Oh, I almost forgot." Jess pulls a soda from her sweater pocket and puts it on the barn floor next to me. "I'll leave you alone out here. I'd want to be alone now, too, if I were you." Jess stands up to leave, but then pauses. "What did you name the kitten?"

120

"Dottie, because she has a dot on her back."

"That name suits her perfectly," she says with a smile. "I'll check on you later." Jess walks out of the pen. She stops at the gate door. "Honey, I truly am sorry." She stares at me for a second. Then she puts her head down and leaves.

Good. I don't feel like talking to Jess or anyone else.

I lay my head on the hay. Please let this be a terrible nightmare. Please.

***

"Anna, it's me Jason. I'm going to carry you to your bedroom. It's dark and you can't sleep in the barn."

Though my eyes are closed, I'm no longer sleeping and can hear Jason talk to Dottie.

"Hey there, Dottie." Jason's voice quivers. "You'll have to stay out here tonight. I'm sure Anna will be out to check on you in the morning."

He lifts her from my arms. I don't open my eyes because I don't want to talk to anyone, and I want him to think I'm sleeping. He lifts me easily and walks to the house. The front door shuts behind us as I float in Jason's arms through the air.

"Is she still sleeping?" Jess asks.

"Yeah, I believe she is. She hasn't opened her eyes the entire time." Jason tries to keep his voice down when he says he's taking me to bed, but I'm still awake.

"She's been in those same pajamas now since yesterday and she's filthy. I wonder if we should change her?"

"Nah, let her sleep. She's been through hell in the last twenty-four hours."

Jason lays me down on my soft bed and then covers me with my blankets. My eyes are still closed, and he has no clue I'm awake. He moves the hair out of my face. My body shifts a little as he sits onto my mattress.

"Sweet, beautiful girl. I am so sorry for what happened to you today. It's wrong—the way they ripped your brother out of your arms. I wish I could take everything back and that your brother was still here." Jason sniffles. "Goodnight, Anna."

My bed springs jump up as Jason's body leaves my mattress. The door clicks shut behind him.

I'm crying again, but quietly. I'm so mad I can feel my heart pounding in my chest. I want to holler and punch anything and everything, including the trees. Every piece of me, right down to my toenails, hurts.

Why did this happen? I try to do something else to try to help me not think about Curtis. That's all I've been doing all day. Sleeping and thinking about Curtis and it hasn't helped me at all. I crawl out of my bed and walk to the window and kneel. I look out into the pasture and see the animals are nowhere to be seen, so they must be in the barn tonight. The bright stars get my attention as I look up.

Jesus, why did you do this? Why?

I go to my desk and pull out paper and a pencil. I don't feel like talking to Jesus right now, so I'll write a letter. Jess bought me paper and a pencil and told me I can write my feelings down one night after Curtis had a fit. I never used it, though, 'til now.

Dear Jesus,

Why did you do this to me? I thought you loved me, but instead, you hurt me just like everybody else has in my life. Why did you take my brother from me? He didn't do anything to you. He didn't even talk to you. He didn't even pray to you. I've been praying to you for weeks to help my brother, and this is how you do it.

I hate you. I'm never going to talk to you again. Never.

I drop the pencil on top of the letter. I squeeze my lips together tight, and my jaw aches. I'm so angry right now.

I shove my fist through the window in my bedroom and glass goes everywhere. I watch the blood run out of my cut-up hand. I feel nothing. I feel no pain. The only pain comes from my heart. The blood drips onto my pink carpet, creating a big circle.

Mahhhm. The sound of the goats jars my mind back to my bedroom and out of my pretend mind. I can almost feel my heart racing when I think about something I want to do but can't. What's different this time is that I'm standing at the window with my fist on the glass. How did I get here? The last thing I remember is writing a letter to Jesus.

My heart beats faster and faster. It feels like it's gonna pop out of my chest and run away. I open my mouth and scream as loud as I can. I don't want to be here. This big fancy house seems scary to me now. I crisscross my arms in front of me. My teardrops fall onto my pajamas, and I start to gag and choke on my tears.

I scream in my head. *"Anna, stop! Anna, shut up!"*

I couldn't stop them from taking my brother. I couldn't stop them from hurting him. I jump up and pace around in my bedroom as I cry out in the worst pain I've ever felt in my entire life. This is worse than stitches. I lean my head against the wall and let my tears fall to the carpet. My anger makes my head and ears hot like a frying pan.

My knuckles burn with extreme pain as I slam my fist into the wall again and again. The pain shoots up to my elbows and into my shoulders. The scream that I held in 'til now echoes through my bedroom like a horn. I shake my head, trying to get the voice in my head to shut up. I didn't protect my brother. That's why he left me. It's my fault. It's all because of me—everything is because of me. We had to leave Daddy because of me. We had to leave the last foster home because of me. Curtis loved Sue. And now, he left today *because of me.*

Why did I have to beat him at rock skipping? Why couldn't I just lose? I'm never gonna throw another rock again. I pound harder and harder on the wall. Blood falls to the floor. I'm never going to throw another—

My bedroom door slams open.

"Anna, stop!" Jason is behind me. "You're going to hurt yourself. Stop!"

I pound harder and harder into the wall. I can't control the anger escaping from me. It won't stop.

Jason wraps his arms around me. He has my arms pinned to my sides as he squeezes.

"Let me go!" I kick harder and harder.

"Anna, it's me, Jason."

I throw my head back. It slams into Jason's face.

I hear Jess gasp. "Jason, you're bleeding all over the place. She must have slammed into your nose."

I never wanted to hurt Jason, yet his grip on me feels like I'm in a cage and cannot get out. I'm just trying to break free. Jess's cries don't stop me from hollering over her words like a wild animal.

"Get me a towel, fast. I can't let her go right now. She's going to do something to seriously hurt herself." Jason sounds hoarse.

I feel something warm and wet in my hair, but it doesn't stop me from trying to get away from him. Jason holding me doesn't stop the pain. It doesn't stop the anger. It doesn't stop anything.

Jess is talking, or rather, she's singing. "Jesus loves me, this I know, for the Bible tells me so…"

I take a deep breath and feel all the muscles in my body relax. I didn't know Jess knew that song. I've never heard her sing it before. I wonder if Curtis taught it to her. The heat in my body turns up, getting hotter and hotter the longer she sings. I explode like a volcano.

"Stop singing that song! I hate Jesus! I hate him! He took my brother away from me! I never want to talk to him again, and I never want to go to his house again! He was supposed to help me! He was supposed to be my friend! Stop singing! I hate him!"

I sob again. Tears fall down my face, and snot runs out of my nose. My eyes are shut tight, and I squint. Not only did I lose my brother today, but I lost Jesus, too. Like all the times before, the room goes blurry and everything turns gray. I almost welcome it, a getaway from the pain if I pass out. I don't feel anything when I'm passed out. That would be nice right now—to feel nothing.

"Anna, sweetheart, calm down. You're hyperventilating again."

***

The birds outside my window wake me. Is it morning already? I wipe my eyes. The sun shines through my bedroom window, and everything outside looks peaceful.

I slowly slide out of bed and sit in my chair with my brother's bear wrapped up in my arms while I rest my head on him. My hands hurt, but I ignore it. This bear is my brother and I'll protect him until I can see my real brother again. Curtis isn't gone forever. It was just another goodbye—but not a *forever* goodbye because he's not dead like Lucky. He's just away for a little bit. I sit in the chair, holding the bear, until someone knocks on my door.

I say nothing. Again, they knock, and again. I don't answer. The door opens slowly.

"Anna? Would you like to come downstairs?"

I shake my head.

Jess's voice is soft. "Honey, you've been in those clothes for days now. We should change them. Maybe, take a bath?"

I do and say nothing except stare out my bedroom window, holding Teddy. Jess's voice fades as my mind drowns it out, and I have no clue what she says.

My bedroom door closes again.

I could answer them, but I'm not going to. I don't want to give them the satisfaction, these people who have destroyed my life by letting Mrs. Alex take my brother. What kind of people do that? If that's what parents do, I'm glad I don't have a mother.

***

I get up and move to my red chair to look out the window. Jess opens my door, this time without saying anything.

"Honey, you've been sitting in that same spot for the past four hours. Would you like to come downstairs to eat?"

I shake my head.

"Okay. Then I'll bring you a sandwich and something to drink."

As promised, she returns with a sandwich and a glass of milk. "I'm going to leave them here on your dresser." Her voice is faint, like everything else in my world right now. It's like I walk around wearing earmuffs.

With that, I am once again alone in my room with my doll and Teddy. My eyes feel bruised because of all the crying I do. Someone turned on the crying switch, and I do not know how to turn it off.

Curtis was that switch. Now, I don't care who sees me cry. I just don't care about anything anymore. Nothing. Soon, Teddy's head is wet. All I can cry is "Currrr… tiss. Currrr… tiss."

Everything outside my window blurs. I stand quickly and drop my brother's bear. Someone's standing by the lake throwing rocks.

Curtis?

I wipe the film off the window so I can see better, ready to sprint downstairs and out the door. The image by the lake fades more and more each time I wipe the window until I can't see anyone anymore.

My shoulders drop in disappointment. Of course it wasn't real. I walk to my bathroom, quietly, because I don't want Jason or Jess to know I'm awake. Once done, I go back to my chair. As before, Teddy and I sit by the window, waiting for Curtis to return.

***

"Anna? I brought you up some dinner." Jess gasps as she walks into the room. "You're still sitting in that hard chair with Curtis's bear? You

125

haven't moved all day? Why don't you lie in your bed? Your bum has to be hurting."

Jess has no idea what she's talking about. My bum stopped hurting this morning. It's completely numb now. All of me is completely numb. She puts her hands on my shoulders. "You can stay up here if you like, but we have to change your clothes. I brought you a clean nightgown instead of the one you've had on for days. I'll leave it by your bed and you can change when I leave. Please consider taking quick shower if you don't want to take a bath. You'll feel better."

I say nothing and do nothing. I stare out the window. I don't think I could respond even if I wanted to.

"Okay, I'm leaving. Let me take—" She gasps again. "You didn't eat your lunch. You didn't drink your milk. Honey, you have to start eating and drinking. If you don't, you'll get sick."

Again, I say and do nothing. I'm not hungry. How can she ask me to eat when all I want to do is sit at this window and hope that I see Curtis come back? I don't care about food. My head throbs with pain and sadness. I want my life back with Curtis in the room next to me.

When I leave my bedroom, I have to walk by his. All it does is make me cry harder to see his empty sailboat room. That reminds me they took him from me.

She stands behind me, doing who-knows-what for a few seconds before she leaves my bedroom. Then, after what feels like forever, I hear the door click shut.

I close my eyes and press my forehead against Teddy. *Curtis, wherever you are, pretend I'm with you. Fight if you must. I* am *with you.* I cry some more until…

***

I can feel my eyelids growing heavy as I drift away into my dream. *I get so excited when I can fly in my dreams. Where do I want to go tonight? I know where—Curtis.*

My arms are stretched open, and I see Curtis below, playing with a bunch of boys at a school building. I fly down to him.

"Anna. You came."

"Of course I did. Do you like it here?"

The scene changes. He's in a room in bed, with a lot of other kids

126

sleeping nearby. "Yeah, it's okay. I get to play basketball every day. I suck, but I'll get better."

"Then why are you crying?"

Curtis fades away, and I can't fly anymore. Instead, someone is putting something over my arms. I can't spread them out to fly. "Stop!" I scream. "Stop!"

"Anna," Jess says. "It's me, honey. You're having a nightmare."

I open my eyes. Jason and Jess are standing over me, and I'm tucked in my bed.

"We couldn't let you sleep in that chair all night. You sat in it all day. You didn't eat or drink anything. You also didn't take care of Dottie. Don't worry, we handled it for you. Twinkles, Sticks, and Black Betty miss you, too." Jason's voice is gentle and calm.

I love my barn friends, but, right now, I don't care about anyone or anything. I'm numb, and everything around me feels dark. It's like I'm at the bottom of a well, and everyone else is standing at the top talking to me, but no one offers me a ladder to help me. No one.

Jason and Jess leave my room. I feel trapped by my blankets. I cry. I want to be with Curtis. I must've fallen asleep again, because the next thing I know, Jess's screams jar me from my sleep as the bedroom door flies open.

It's not until I hear Jess's screams that my eyes open.

"There's blood everywhere. Jason, get up here and bring my medical bag. Anna? Anna? What did you do? What did you do?"

Chapter 17
Pastor Chad

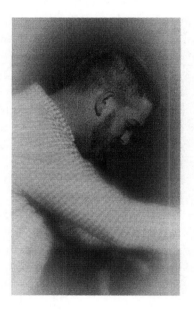

The pain in my arm rockets through me and, for a minute, takes away the ache in my heart. I don't want to be here anymore. I don't want this life anymore. This world is eating me slowly. The sharp stabs shot signals up my arm to wake me up. My eyes fight against the demands and stay closed.

When I finally get them to open, blood's everywhere, and Curtis's bedroom window is broken.

"This is going to hurt." Jessica holds up a white towel. "I need to stop the bleeding so I can see if you need stitches."

I scream out in pain as she wraps a white cloth around my upper arm and ties it tight.

"Anna? Did you punch your brother's window? Did you put your arm through it? You have cuts all over your arm and wrist."

Everything is happening so fast, I don't know how to answer her questions.

Jason brings in her black bag. "Here, honey." His eyes burn a hole through me, but I don't care what he wants to know.

I want to know why he let them take my brother, but he hasn't come up with a good enough answer—because there isn't one. He made Mrs. Alex take my brother. I'm never talking to Jason again.

Jess rips open a small packet and pulls something out of it and wipes my skin. It feels cool against me. She then pulls out a needle, removes the lid, and flicks it with her fingers. A drop of liquid comes out of the tip. "I'm not going to lie to you. This is going to hurt, but I promise it won't last long," she says. "Jason, hold her tight. I can't have her jumping around when the needle's in her arm."

Jason gently pins me to Curtis' bed, and my bleeding arm is stretched to the side. "Look at me and not at Jessica, Anna."

The room swims around me. Jessica shoves a needle into my arm with all the cuts. If Jason wasn't holding me, I'd be jumping off of the bed. Whatever's in that needle burns the entire way to my shoulder.

"Give it a second and you won't feel any pain. This needle makes the pain go away so I can clean the cuts and check them to see if they need stitches." Jessica holds my arm across her lap. "Thanks, Jason," she says. "You can let go of her now if she promises to hold still. You promise, Anna?"

I bite my lip and nod, too frightened to consider doing anything else. He releases me and listens as Jessica tells him to go get something. I can't focus on what she's saying. I feel like I'm underwater. She pulls some cloth out of her bag and then rubs my fingers. "Can you feel that?"

I shake my head as my lip trembles. It's an odd sensation to see her rubbing my skin but I can't feel a thing. It feels almost like when I fall asleep on my arm, and it won't work for a few minutes. It's like my entire body is numb. It's been like this since Curtis left. I'm only going to feel again when he comes back to me.

Jason comes back into the room, breathing fast. He has a bowl in his hands.

Jess squeezes my hand. "Anna, I'm going to tell you everything I'm doing. Though you won't feel anything, I don't want you to get scared. I need to clean your cuts and decide if they need stitches. You were bleeding pretty good when we came in. It's slowing down now, so I can loosen this cloth I tied around your arm so I can see your cuts."

From here, everything moves quickly. I don't feel anything, as promised, but a bunch of tugging feelings. Before I know it, she's done cleaning my wounds, and she put some tiny bandages across three of my cuts. Then, she uses a lot of gauze to clean my arm.

"Done. Let's sit you up slowly. You won't feel any pain in this arm right now, but you will in about an hour. Don't move these little bandages 'til I tell you to." Her voice is stern.

Once I'm sitting up, I see that my brother's bedroom window is indeed broken again and glass is all over the window ledge and the floor. They just had that window fixed a few days ago.

"What happened in here?" Jason stands, watching Jess.

It takes me a second to remember, and even then, I don't trust my memory. It's like the morning was foggy. "I came into Curtis' bedroom this morning because I thought I heard him calling my name. When I got in here, I saw that he wasn't here. Then I heard him calling my name from outside the window. I swear he was sitting outside the window on the roof. We liked to do that sometimes when you didn't know about it. But, I couldn't get the window open. I tried to push up on the window to get it to move when... I fell through it."

"Why didn't you yell for us?" Jessica's words were full of worry.

"I don't know. I don't remember anything else 'til you busted into the room, screaming when I was lying on his bed. I thought I was still in my room. I'm really confused."

"Honey, are you sure you didn't do this on purpose to hurt yourself?"

I barely remember any of it. It felt like a dream. "I don't think so. It feels like all of it was a dream." This isn't a lie. The entire time, I felt like I was sleeping.

"Okay. It sounds like a nightmare. Do you have a lot of them? Her voice is as clear as a bell while she speaks.

I shrug. "I don't know. All I know is that I heard Curtis calling my name, so I wanted to find him."

Jessica rubs my back. "Okay. Well then, it sounds like you were having a nightmare and sleepwalking at the same time. Let me see your arm again. I want to make sure the bleeding stops before I wrap it all up in a bandage. I also called in an antibiotic for you. We need to make sure you don't get an infection in that arm, so I'll check it again later. I didn't see any glass in your cuts. One looked like it might be on the verge of needing stitches, but I thought maybe we could try the strips first." She smiles. "Let's get you up and move around." She lifts me off the bed. "You sat all day yesterday. Let's get you moving a little today."

I stand and see that my brother's bear has blood on it by the window. I yell out. "My brother's bear. I got blood on it."

"I see that. Don't worry, I can get that blood out. Don't pick up the bear now because we need to make sure there's glass in it." Jessica sounds kind,

"I think most of the glass went outside when her arm went through the window," Jason examines the glass on the floor and on the roof. "I'll clean it for you, Anna, so you'll have your brother's bear back."

"Jessica?" I wait for her to answer.

"Yes?"

"I don't feel good and I'm exhausted. Can I go to bed with my doll?"

"Okay. but I want you up later today, eating something and walking around. Deal?"

I nod because all I care about is being alone because my body still has tears that need to get out. As I leave my brother's bedroom, I look back. Blood is all over Curtis' light blue sheet and on the side of his white bed. "I got blood on my brother's bed. Will you clean it, Jessica, for when he comes back?"

One of her eyebrows lifts while the other stays in place. "Um… sure. I can do that for you, but let's get you to bed for now." Jessica guides me to my room.

I roll into bed, while Jason pulls the shades and Jessica tucks the fluffy, white blanket around my doll and me.

"Good night, Curtis." I whisper.

***

Jessica comes into the room and raises my blinds. It's bright out. I musta slept all night.

"We have someone here who would like to talk with you, Anna. I can help you get up and around. I'm going to the bathroom, and I can be back to check your arm and help you downstairs." She leaves the room.

I know Jess cares about me, and I know she didn't mean to hurt me. Deep down, I know she cared about Curtis, too. But, I can't help being so angry. It doesn't sound like I have a choice. I sit up on the edge of my bed and wait for Jessica.

"Okay, let's head downstairs. I'll hold your arm. You haven't eaten anything or drank anything for two days now. It's not an option. You need to eat and drink."

I hear a man's voice coming from the kitchen, talking with Jason, as I reach the bottom step. "Who's here?" I ask.

"You'll see."

I panic, thinking it's someone who works with Mrs. Alex, but I'm too tired to fight right now.

"Anna, let's sit down, and I need you to drink the water on the table." Jessica pulls the chair out for me. The kitchen table has a bowl of potato chips, dips, cheese, and crackers.

A strange man looks at me. "Hello, Anna. I am Pastor Chad. The Tubners asked me to come talk with you because of what happened with your brother." The strange man opens the letter that I wrote to Jesus.

"I'm sorry to spring this on you, Anna. I thought our pastor could help. We saw you wrote a letter to Jesus, and you're mad at him." Jess kneels down next to my chair, her voice gentle as she suggests that Pastor Chad could help me.

Pastor Chad flashes me a smile. "I am here to help in any way I can." He looks like a teenager with his hair combed to the side.

"You're a pastor?" I ask.

"Yes, I am."

"Jesus is your friend?"

Pastor Chad takes a brief pause. "I guess you can say that, but he is also my father, just like he's yours." He holds his finger up as if it were pointing towards Jesus.

"I remember people saying that in my old church, too. But Jesus is—was—my friend, that is." I put my head down. My heart hurts. "Jesus didn't help my brother. He made him go away. Jesus took Curtis from me." My gaze stays locked on the table in front of me.

"Mmmm, I see. Did you pray for Jesus to help your brother?" The pastor leans closer to me.

I answer quickly. "Yes, I did. Every night when I talked with Jesus, I asked him to help my brother."

132

Pastor Chad nods. "You asked Jesus to help your brother every night."

He repeats what I said and I don't understand why. "Yes, I did."

"Anna?" He puts his hand on mine on the table. "How do you know that Jesus didn't answer your prayers and help your brother? How do you know moving Curtis is not helping him?"

I snap my head up and wish I could shoot daggers from my eyes. "Because he took him from me. How can it help my brother to be away from me? I was always the one protecting him. It was me."

"Dear child, you may be right about that, but when you asked Jesus to help your brother, you asked him to take over. You no longer had to protect your brother because you asked Jesus to do that, right?"

I nod. My mind is blank, and I'm struggling to think of something to say. This guy knows Jesus better than me since he teaches everyone about him.

"Maybe Jesus thought the best way to help your brother was to find him a place that could help him. And, sadly for you, maybe that place doesn't include you right now."

I stare down at the table once more. Did Jesus really take my brother away from me to help him? I wouldn't want to go to an all-boys home. So, if he had to go there to get help, I guess then Jesus knows what he is doing.

"Anna, I want to ask you a question. Is that okay? Do you think you can tell me the truth?"

I hesitate. Then I nod.

"Has your brother killed cats in the past?"

I'm speechless. After a few seconds, I clear my throat and whisper, "Yes."

"This may be Jesus's way of helping your brother. He's in a home where professionally trained people can help him stop killing animals. Isn't that what you asked Jesus to do—to help stop Curtis from hurting animals?"

I look up at him again and nod.

"So, I think Jesus *did* answer your prayers. Curtis is now getting the help he needs. During this difficult time, prayers to Jesus can help your sadness. Remember, your brother is alive. You will see him again someday, hopefully soon. He's just getting the help he needs."

"Jesus is helping my brother?" I ask.

"Yes. I think Jesus answered your prayer and is helping your brother now."

For the first time in a while, my stomach doesn't hurt, and I feel a little better. Maybe Jesus *is* trying to help me by helping my brother like I asked him to do.

Pastor Chad stays for dinner, and I eat the small sandwich Jessica made for me. I feel better about Jesus helping my brother and I'm no longer mad at him. I'm still sad and miss Curtis, though. I take the last bite of my sandwich. "Jessica? Can I go to bed? I'm tired."

She puts the dish in the dishwasher and looks at me. "Do you want to go visit Dottie tonight?"

"No, I'm really tired. Can you feed her for me, please?"

The slump of Jessica's shoulders shows her sadness. "Jason is taking care of Dottie. You don't have to worry."

I'm sad. I can't take care of Dottie. It seems that all I can do is to be sad. I don't have the energy to do anything else but sit in my chair.

"Go on, head upstairs. I'll check on you later. If your arm starts to ache, come find me and I'll give you something for the pain, okay?"

"Thanks, Jessica." I pull away from the table and head upstairs. As I approach my brother's bedroom door, I can feel the lump return to my throat. I go into his cleaned-up room, now with no traces of blood, and lie on his bed. Jason must have cleaned last night and put plastic over the window.

Jess said I could go to her if the pain becomes too much. Well, the pain's been bad for days now and there is nothing she can do to fix it.

Jesus, I'm sorry that I said I hate you and would never talk to you again. Thank you for helping my brother. But next time, I am going to ask you to help him with him living with me. Please help me not be so sad. My heart hurts, and I can't make it stop. Please help me feel better. "Leave him alone. Leave him alone!" I scream at Mrs. Alex as loud as I can. Curtis is being pulled from me, so I grab his hand.

"Anna, don't let go!"

I scream for my brother. I blink, and he's gone. I keep screaming his name. "Cur... tisss!"

"Anna, wake up. It's me, Jessica. Please. You're having a nightmare again."

I open my eyes. I'm standing at the top of the stairs, and Jason, once again, has his arms wrapped around me. "How did I get here?"

Jason's voice is a whisper coming from behind me. "We don't know. We came out of our bedroom to hear you screaming and leaning over the railing with your arms out, calling for your brother. Then you ran to the top of the staircase and acted like you were going to jump."

Every part of me is shaking.

"Were you dreaming about Curtis again?" Jessica sounds afraid.

I nod.

Jessica comes over to me. "Release her, Jason. I don't want you hurting her sore arm." Jessica puts her hand on my shoulder. "Follow me. Tonight, you're sleeping in our room."

She has blankets and a pillow on the couch in their bedroom. "Jason, lock our door. If she sleepwalks again, we need to know."

"Anna, here's to a good night's sleep. Try to get some rest," Jessica says.

I say good night to each of them. I don't enjoy sleeping in her bedroom, but I don't have a choice.

***

"It's been the same thing now for weeks."

Jessica doesn't know I'm sitting on the steps and can hear Jason and her talking.

"She's supposed to start school, and she can't make it through a night without having a nightmare. We are not getting any sleep either. Jason, what are we going to do?"

135

Chapter 18
The Ride

"I know you don't want to hear this, but Mrs. Alex says this house may be a trigger for the trauma of losing her brother."

What does that mean—trigger for my trauma? I have the same type of dream every night—always something to do with Curtis. It's been a while since he left, but it's not any easier living here without him. I was supposed to start school this week, but I refused to leave my room so Jessica didn't make me.

Though I check on my new kitty every day, I'm too sad to spend too much time with her still. I wonder if this is what Jessica means when she talks about trauma. Does trauma mean I'm sad? If that is what it means, then Jessica is one hundred percent right because I'm sad all the time. My heart hurts all the time. I cry all the time. And, I'm tired all the time.

Jessica's voice brings me out of my own head to listen to what she and Jason are talking about. I sit on the steps a little longer.

"She has a hard time every night here and every day. She cries every day. When she walks by his bedroom, she cries. She has to sleep in our room most of the time just so we can feel she's safe, knowing she won't go through a window or fly down the stairs if she's with us—"

"I hear you, Jessica, but how do we do this? I'm going to take care of the animals and milk the cows. I can't have this conversation with Mrs. Alex, I just can't. That woman…" He sighs. "Let me know how your conversation goes and what's the best thing for Anna. I'll support whatever decision is made for that little girl no matter how hard it is for me, as long as it's good for her."

I hear Jason's footsteps echoing in the foyer as he moves to go outside, so I quickly jump up and make a dash for my bedroom. What are they talking about? Why are they going to speak with Mrs. Alex? My gut doesn't feel good, and I have a terrible feeling again. Anytime I hear Mrs. Alex's name, I immediately want to throw up. That woman does nothing but come to move us. She doesn't care about foster kids at all.

I grab Teddy and sit in my red chair in front of the window. Like all the other days for the past weeks, I wait for Curtis to return. Maybe, today, Jessica will ask Mrs. Alex to bring my brother back since she's going to talk with her later. I watch the birds flying outside, chasing each other from one tree to another. My bum is so used to sitting on this little, red chair most days that it doesn't hurt anymore.

The sound of a boat horn echoes across the lake. I know it's not Jason's because it sounds like it's whizzing by. Tears slide down my cheek, something I've gotten used to. It feels like those tears are tiny boats, sailing down a stream to my lips. I'm familiar with the taste now.

Curtis loves boats but never had the opportunity to go on Jason's. If only he had given this place a chance, I know he would've liked it here. I know I did, like it here, that is, 'til Mrs. Alex stole Curtis from me. Now everything around here reminds me of him and I… hate that. I hate feeling sad all the time and no matter how much I try it doesn't get better.

Jess and Jason are really great foster parents, and they always ask how I am and what they can do to help me. Sadly, the one thing I need they can*not* do—bring back Curtis.

What are you doing today, Curtis? What kind of things are you

137

doing at your new home? I'm sitting here waiting for you to come back to me. Jesus is helping you now because I asked him. So, I hope you're feeling better. I'll always wait for you.

I close my eyes and rest my head on his bear. *I love you, Curtis. Where are you? Are you okay?* You must come back to me. I don't want to live anymore if you aren't in my life.

***

"Anna, can I come in?"

I don't know why Jessica bothers. She's already opened my bedroom door a little—which she's done for the past few weeks now. Like, it's not even my bedroom anymore. First, they take my brother, now they're taking my room. Nothing is mine.

"Yeah."

"Honey, I need to talk to you about something important. Can you look at me for a second?"

I really don't want to. I don't care about anything but Curtis. I hug his bear closer and then look up. "What?"

"I had a conversation today with Mrs. Alex. Jason and I are worried about you. Since your brother left, all you do is sit in your chair all day, holding the bear. You barely eat or drink unless I stand over you and make you. Honey, I think you're seriously depressed. I also think that living in this house makes it harder to move forward because there are so many memories of Curtis." Jessica sniffles. "Jason and I want you to be happy and we don't feel you can be happy *here*. We've talked with Mrs. Alex, and she's decided that the best place for you may be somewhere where there are no memories of Curtis." Jessica sniffles some more.

So, I'm being moved again.

I stare at Jessica but don't speak as a tear tracks down my cheek. I want to say a lot, but I'm too tired and sad to care to say it. My body feels like it's sleeping, and I can't wake it up. I don't want to leave this foster home, but I have no energy to fight it.

"Anna, do you understand what I am saying to you?" She asks with tears in her eyes. "I'm sorry, honey. We don't know how to help you. You sit here every day wasting away and you won't let us love you or care for you." Jess wipes the tear off her cheek. "I think this house reminds you of your brother too much. Please know if we could do anything else to help and keep you here, we would." Jess breaks out in a full sob.

I listen to her cry for a minute. I really don't want her to be sad.

"I'm sorry, Anna." Jess stands by my chair.

I nod and then close my eyes again, put my head on the bear, and block out everything. It's another move. Maybe someday soon, I can get used to this, so it's easier. Move from one family to another and to another. I should be sad, and maybe I am and don't know it. Nothing can hurt me worse than that awful day with Curtis. I shiver when I think and feel Curtis' hands being torn away from my neck, and for a minute… I swear I can hear him throwing a fit in his bedroom.

I was crossing my fingers that Jess and Jason would get Curtis back, but that didn't happen. Jason and Jessica are great people, but I don't want to hear Curtis's voice coming from an empty bedroom anymore.

Before too long, I hear the click of my bedroom door. Phew. She's gone. I feel relieved because I don't enjoy hearing her sadness. She's a nice person. I don't think Jess and Jason could help Curtis either, because he was so mad. I won't let them help me. This place makes me feel sad with all the memories of Curtis.

Jesus, please make sure Jessica and Jason are not sad. They're nice people and have been nice to me. I want to stay here with them, but maybe at the next foster home, Curtis can come back to me. But please take care of my brother and make sure he's safe before he can come back. I can't be away from him much longer. So please hurry up and do what you got to do to fix him. Without him, who is going to love me? Who?

***

My eyes pop open when I hear the nasty engine of Mrs. Alex's car as it pulls up the driveway. Mrs. Alex gets out wearing an ugly, brown dress that goes to the ground. She looks like she always does with her thick, black glasses and hair going everywhere, looking like the wicked witch she is. I hear the front door close, so I run to the hallway to sit against the staircase railing so I can hear them talk.

"Hello, Jessica and Jason. Is Anna ready to go?"

"I believe she's in her bedroom."

I'm not in my bedroom.

"How's she doing?" Mrs. Alex's voice is loud. It's always loud.

139

"Well, since Curtis left, the only thing we hear is her crying in her sleep or when she walks by his bedroom." Jessica starts to cry. "She changed after that day. She doesn't go to the barn anymore. She barely eats and spends all day in her room. We've tried everything to help her. We worry that she's getting increasingly sad, and being here might be a big trigger for her."

"Does she know she's leaving?" Mrs. Alex asks.

"When I told her earlier today, she didn't respond. The only emotion I saw was a tear sliding down her face. That's it." Jessica's whispered speech is dotted with sniffles.

"Is there anything else you think we can do for her here? Are there any counselors or anyone around here?" Jason asks.

I sit slumped against the railing. In my head, I'm screaming and want to fight the decision to leave, but I'm slumped over with my brother's bear, and I just don't care. I simply don't care about anything.

"Let me go ahead and get her stuff in the car. Anna is not a simple move. I have backup that should arrive soon." Mrs. Alex sounds so cold when she talks about me. It's like I'm not even a person, but a thing.

"Backup?" Jason asks.

"Yes, I called the local police for help, just like we had to do with Curtis. I've moved that child five times since she was born. Three times in the last year and a half. It's never been easy moving her. When I first moved her from her birth mother at eighteen months, even then, she stood in the back seat, pounding at the rear window. So yes, I called for backup."

She's now talking to them how she always talks to me. She's just mean. I sneak closer to the end of the wall so I can peek around the corner and see what's going on downstairs.

There's a knock at the door. Jessica opens it, and there stands a police officer.

"Hey, Mrs. Alex, I'm here to help move Anna."

The man in the blue suit knows my name. Mrs. Alex hands him a garbage bag.

I tilt my head because I don't remember Jessica packing my room. I stand up quietly, leaving my bear on the hallway floor and run back into my room. I open each drawer as quietly as I can—yup, they're all empty. She must've packed them up when I was sleeping last night. I grab my doll off the bed and then go back into the hallway to grab Teddy.

It's time to go. We have to leave. *I'm sorry, Teddy. You'll get used to it just like my doll and I are.* I kiss Teddy's head and walk down the steps. On the third step everyone in the foyer turns and looks at me. I take the last few steps to the foyer, carrying the last two important things I have left in my life.

I look at Jason. "Goodbye, Jason. Thank you for being nice and please take care of Dottie. Give Black Betty, Twinkles, and Sticks a hug, too, and tell them I will miss them."

Jason cries as he gives me and my friends a big bear hug.

When he finally lets go, I look at Jessica. "Goodbye, Jessica. Thank you for fixing my arm and letting me sleep in your bedroom with you at night when I had a nightmare."

Jessica cries louder than Jason. She walks over to me and does the same thing as Jason. "My sweet girl, remember how strong you are. Don't forget you can become whatever you want to be in your life. Foster care doesn't mean that you're broken or damaged. Please remember that." She kisses the top of my head before she lets go.

I look at the police officer. "I don't need you today, so you can go home."

The officer smiles. "Well, thank you."

I look at Mrs. Alex. "I'll wait for you in the car."

Her mouth hangs open as I walk by her, carrying my brother's bear and my doll. I stop just as I step by her and turn around. "You better close your mouth. We have a lot of flies here on the farm."

She glares at me but pushes her lips together tight.

I then walk out the door and down the sidewalk. The officer runs by me. "I'll open the door for you. You seem like a strong young lady. If you ever need anything, call the police and ask for Officer Jim."

As he's talking with me, another police car shows up and a woman officer gets out of the vehicle.

"Hello, Officer Deb."

"Hello, Jim. How's it going today?"

"Good. I don't think we're going to need your assistance today. Miss Anna Snow is in control of this move today." He smiles at me.

"Hello, Anna. You remind me of me when I was little. Tough and strong. Remember that. Before you know it, you'll be all grown up and out of this system. Don't stop fighting, and fight for what you want in this life." She rubs the top of my head. "Girl power." She puts her hand up, and I give her a high-five.

These officers are so much nicer than the ones who moved Curtis, but maybe that's because I'm not kicking or screaming at them. I slide into the back seat next to my garbage bag as Mrs. Alex walks in front of the car.

"Thank you for coming. I'm shocked. This is the easiest move so far with this young lady. Have a wonderful day," Mrs. Alex sounds so cheerful with the police. She's so fake. She gets into the driver's seat, turns the engine on, and then takes me away from yet another foster home.

This is just another goodbye. I have to remember that. I've done this before and it doesn't have to be horrible. I have to remind myself, the worst things that ever could happen to me already did. My brother, Daddy, and Thunder, they were the three worst days of my entire life. No matter what happens from now on, I will be okay.

I wave to Jason, who has his arm around Jessica. Both of them are crying.

Goodbye, Jessica.

Goodbye, Jason.

Goodbye, Dottie.

Goodbye, Black Betty.

Goodbye, Twinkles.

Goodbye, Sticks.

And goodbye to all the sad memories of my brother.

The car turns right, going out of the driveway. I hug my brother's bear. I'm not alone in this car—Curtis is with me because I have his bear.

I close my eyes and hope that the next foster home will have a horse and that they will bring my brother back to me after I get there.

All of this is just another goodbye.

Chapter 19
A Note

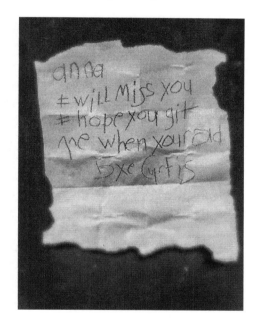

Things in the car are quiet at first, which is nice. I lean my head on Teddy and watch as another world disappears. All the things I saw on the way to this foster home, the roads, the houses, and the trees, are left behind.

I glance over at my garbage bag. It's so weird to see only one. For a second, I pretend I can feel my brother's arms wrapped around my waist as he sits close to me. *Where are we going? When will we get there? What do you think the family will be like?* All of his questions used to frustrate me because I didn't have answers for him. Now, I'd give anything to hear him asking me those questions.

Curtis, I miss you.

The car jerks to a stop and I fly into the back of the seat in front of me, then slide to the floor.

"Holy crap!" Mrs. Alex yells as I scramble back into my seat. "That darn car stopped with no warning. Anna, are you okay?" She turns to watch me settle back into my seat.

I pull Teddy and my doll onto my lap. "Yeah." I don't look at her. How can I? This awful lady took my brother from me.

The car moves again. "Tonight, when I get home, I think I'm going to make spaghetti for dinner. I haven't had that in a while."

Why does this lady always talk about food every time we're in the car?

"Anna?"

I look up and see her face in the little mirror.

"Do you like spaghetti?"

She's *seriously* asking if I like spaghetti? Why? She's going home to her perfect, little house and her perfect, little family to make her perfect, little spaghetti for dinner, when I get to go to some new stranger's house with people I don't know and only a doll and a teddy bear to share it with. Did she ask *Curtis* if he likes spaghetti when she ripped him from me and drove away? Does she even care if he does?

Does she even care if I do? Of course she doesn't. We're just garbage bag people to her. But, to us, we're the only family either one has.

I know my brother. I bet he was scared to death in this car. Even these crayons and paper she's put back here wouldn't make him un-scared. "What are the crayons and paper for?"

"Good question." She smiles as big as she can into her mirror.

I don't like her smile. And I don't like her.

"It's something new I have in the car for kids to use on the long rides to someplace new." She continues to smile.

"Did my brother use it?"

Her smile goes away. "Um… yes, I believe he did."

"What did he make?" I want to know. I *need* to know to feel like he's with me.

"It looked like he was writing a note."

"A note to who?"

"Anna, I don't know for sure. All I could see was that he was writing letters on a paper. I can't tell you any more than that."

"Where did you take my brother? I want to know."

Mrs. Alex doesn't answer me, but, instead, turns up the radio and sings along to a song I've never heard before. I try to tune her out.

When Curtis and I lived in our first foster home, we wrote messages to each other and would leave them under rocks for each of us to find. *I wonder...* Mrs. Alex turns down the radio. Desperate to find a clue, I move around in the back seat, hoping to find a scrap of paper that Curtis has left.

"What're you doing back there? You act like the seat's hot and it's burning your bum. You need to sit still while I'm driving. I don't want to get distracted and end up off the road like we did before."

I ignore her and keep searching. I pull out a half-eaten lollipop from between the seats. Eww, gross. I throw it on the car floor and keep searching. I know my brother would've left me a note if he could. I know it.

"Mrs. Alex?"

She responds quickly. "Yeah?"

"What side of the car did Curtis sit on?"

She doesn't say anything for a second. I'm afraid she'll turn the radio back up and ignore me, so I make up something fast. "I just want to sit on the same side he did, that's all."

"I understand. He sat behind me."

I quickly kick my garbage bag to the floor and slide over behind Mrs. Alex.

"Anna, what the heck was that?"

"Nothing, I just moved my garbage bag."

I dig between the seats. I find four pennies—and then... *paper.* Something sharp scrapes my fingers as I pull it out from under the seat. It's only the lollipop wrapper. My excitement fades. The lollipop wrapper feels tacky against my hands. The feeling of sadness creeps over my shoulders and weighs me down. My tears trickle down. I don't want Mrs. Alex to see or hear what I'm doing. I would be so happy if... But, maybe he was too sad to even think about it. I sit back in my seat and hug his Teddy.

Mrs. Alex hits a bump and I jump up in my seat. Then, I see a section of the seat I didn't check. I didn't search the crease in the seat by the window. I lean down then shove my hand in.

Aha!

I hold my breath in case it's another wrapper.

But… it's not. It's white, like the kind in the notebook on the floor. I hide it as I drag it across the seat so Mrs. Alex doesn't see it. I open it.

Anna. I will miss you. I hope you git me when yore old. Curtis.

I trace his letters as a tear falls onto the paper. I'm definitely going to get my brother sooner than when I'm old.

"What're you doing back there, Anna? Would you like to stop and get something to eat?"

Really? This woman wants me to stop and have a cheeseburger with her. I punch the back of her seat. Just like Curtis did when we were last in this car together. It feels kinda nice, actually. Now I get why he did it.

"What was that?" she asks.

"Nothing. Um… I moved my foot and accidentally kicked the back of your seat." I shove Curtis's note into my back pocket.

"Do you want to grab something to eat?"

I bite my lip. "No. Just take me to wherever you're taking me. Let's get there already." It's always scary going to a new house. You don't know if you're getting someone nice like Jess, Jason, or Daddy, or mean like Derek or Sue. The taste of blood stings my mouth.

"Okay, but if you change your mind, let me know because I'm going to stop and get something for myself."

Ugh. I say nothing, but my lip takes the brunt of my anger as I bite down harder.

After Mrs. Alex feeds her face, she jumps in the car licking her nasty lips like always. "Maybe one of these trips you'll actually want to get something to eat." This lady is going crazy. I will never eat with her on one of these trips.

I close my eyes when I realize… Mrs. Alex just mentioned that there would be more trips. Great. She expects to move me around forever. What a horrible thought. Quickly, the sunlight outside feels dark.

"We're here." Her voice pierces my ear drum.

Another foster home.

"We're here."

I open my eyes. I hadn't been sleeping, I just didn't want to watch another move happen. I look out the window and my mouth drops open. I must look like Mrs. Alex did when I got in her car without fussing.

The house is missing some red paint, shingles are falling off the roof, and an upstairs window has tape on it.

I don't move. "Are you sure this is the right place?"

"Yep, it is. Let's get moving, I don't have all day. This is the home of Dorsey Strudder. She takes only teenage girls."

"I'm not a teenager," I say, refusing to move.

"You're close enough." She slams her car door shut and opens mine. "Let's get going. You can't sit in the car all day. I have another child I have to move, and it's getting late. I'd like to be home before it's dark. So, can we move it, please?"

A girl with messy, black hair and food all over her face runs to the car. "Is this the new girl? Is it? Is it?" She jumps in Mrs. Alex's face.

"Yes, Catrina, this is the new girl." Mrs. Alex pushes her back a little. "Catrina, I need you to move back so I can open the door." Mrs. Alex pushes her lips together. "Come on, Anna, let's get out."

This place looks worse than any place I've lived in. I grab my bear and garbage bag in one hand and then tuck my doll, who I call Rags, under my arm. As soon as I'm out of the car, Catrina is in my face like she was with Mrs. Alex a minute ago.

"I love your doll. Can I have it? Can I?"

I can't walk any further because she's so close that our noses almost touch. Her breath smells like dead fish. I step back. I can't do this. What kind of place is this?

"Catrina," a voice yells from the house. "Move your ass away from her and let her come in. Get in here!"

The girl finally moves away from my face. The owner of the screaming voice steps out of the house. She has a pointy, black hat that sits tall on her head and her long, black hair comes out of the bottom. Her long, green dress goes to the ground and has a rope looking thing tied around it at her hips.

Oh my gosh, she's a witch!

Her eyes grow wider as she studies us. "I thought she was coming tomorrow." She turns to Catrina, "Hey, honey, why don'tcha go into da house. Make room for da new girl." This time, her voice sounds sweet.

I study her face. She has a huge nose and no teeth.

"Catrina, git da other girls down here so they can meet her."

Catrina puts her head down and runs inside. Mrs. Alex pushes me to the door and then inside. My stomach hurts as what sounds like a thunderstorm lets loose in the house—a house that smells worse than Jessica and Jason's barn.

Holy crap! No. Get me out of here.

Seven girls—besides Catrina—run down the stairs. I'm not ready for this. They knock each other over running into a dirty, disgusting living room where there's—ohmygosh—a PILE OF POOP in the corner. And I thought an old lollipop was gross? Who has poop in their living room? I cannot live here. I'd rather live in the barn with Sticks.

"That darn dog just pooped before you two got here." The foster mother must have caught me looking at it. "It's my sista's dog. She picked up that damn disgusting thing right before yas git here. It must've left us a mess."

The witch glares at me while Mrs. Alex is busy talking with another girl. "Catrina. Get a towel and pick up that poop."

Catrina moves fast, doing as she's told.

Mrs. Alex puts her hand on my shoulder and, for once, I don't want to shake it off. She's even a better option than the witch.

"Everyone, I want you to meet Anna."

A girl with long, blonde hair stares at me. "She looks fancy in her white sandals, nice blue jeans, and pretty blue-and-white top. Is she rich or something?" She tosses her hair to the side and scrunches her face at Mrs. Alex. "Well, is she?"

Mrs. Alex shakes her head. "No, Nisa, she's a foster child just like you, so be nice to her."

A girl with short, brown hair and black skin, who's holding a book in her hand, says, "She looks too fancy to be one of us."

"Liz, I assure you, she's a foster child," Mrs. Alex says.

The longer I stand with everyone staring at me the dirtier I feel. It's like I'm standing in a glass bowl and can't move. Everyone else can though as they walk around me in circles.

That's what I feel like now standing in this nasty disgusting room. The carpet, I think, is supposed to be green, but it's all black in some spots and the sofa looks super old and ripped up. Everything here looks gross.

"Hello, Anna. Welcome. I'm Dorsey Strudder." She pats the furniture for me to sit down.

"I don't need to sit on the sofa, I'm fine standing up." I don't think I'm *ever* going to need to sit on that sofa. It's disgusting. So different from Jessica and Jason's home.

The girls laugh.

"Did you just hear her fancy talk?" one of them asks loudly.

Nisa flips her hair back again and walks over to the sofa. "No, thank you, Mrs. Dorsey. I don't need to sit on that there soffffaaa." She turns and sits down.

I don't understand why Nisa seems to hate me, and why she likes flipping her hair around so much. Is that a teenager thing? Will I have to do that someday?

"Knock it off, Nisa, and help her take her stuff to her bed," Mrs. Dorsey says.

The hell she is. No one is touching my stuff. I tighten my grip on my bear, doll, and garbage bag. Nisa comes over and reaches for my bag.

I jerk my hand away. "I've got it," I say, snarling.

"Woooooow," all the girls say.

"No need to be rude, child. Little Nisa is only trying to help ya." Mrs. Dorsey stares at me. I glare back.

Mrs. Alex clears her throat. "Yes, well, I'm sure it'll all work out, now come introduce yourselves."

"Before you all disappear, introduce yourself to Anna Snow," Mrs. Alex says.

"Even her name is fancy," someone says from the group of girls.

My head swings everywhere looking at everything going on. I don't even know who said it. I'm too overwhelmed to care. So many people live in one house. I hope one of these girls will want to be my friend.

I swear my new, white sandals are getting dirty just standing on the sticky carpet. The smell in here makes me feel like I want to throw up. What have I done? I had a nice foster home that was clean and fancy with people who cared for me. I want to go back to Jess and Jason. My heart races as fast as my thoughts.

"Mrs. Alex." I turn to her and whisper. "I want to go back to Jess and Jason."

She glares at me and scrunches her eyes together. "That will never happen. So get used to it." She smirks. I so want to punch her ugly old face. There's no way around it. This is going to be my new home.

The girl with dark hair and skin holds her hand out to me. I shake it.

"Hi. I'm Liz. I've lived here for a few months now. Nice to meet you, Anna Snow." She lets go and walks toward the stairs.

Then someone else grabs my hand while I watch Liz walk away.

"Hi. Immmma Caaaatttrinnnnaa." The girl from the driveway stands so close I swear she's going to kiss me. I jump back.

149

"Move it, moron. No one cares who you are." Nisa mocks her.

Catrina's shoulders slump. I squeeze her hand back. "Hello, Catrina. It's nice to meet you. I'm Anna Snow." I smile at her and she does the same.

"Eww, now you have Catrina cooties all over your hands." Nisa acts like she is trying to make herself laugh.

I press my arm against my side so my doll doesn't drop out from under it, then hold out my hand to Nisa—the same one Catrina touched. "Hello. My name is Anna Snow."

Nisa doesn't take it.

"Take her hand and shake it! Ya ain't gonna be rude in this house!" Mrs. Dorsey sounds like a grumpy, old woman.

Slowly, Nisa takes my hand and shakes it.

I smile at her and whisper, "Now you're the one with cooties."

Nisa rips her hand out of mine. "You wait, prissy girl. You're gonna get yours. You just wait." Nisa's hair flairs as she turns and leaves the living room.

Mrs. Dorsey's lips are pressed together so hard wrinkles form around them.

"Yo. I'm Tori." This girl has a deep voice that sounds like a boy's and her red hair, cut short, looks like a boy's too. It's cut short and parted on the side. "Ignore that bitch, Nisa. She just thinks she's hot." Tori winks at me and walks away to go upstairs. I wouldn't mess with Tori. She looks tough, like she has muscles everywhere. Her tattoos go all over her arms and she has bracelets of string going up to her elbows. She definitely looks scary. I'm glad she's acting nice to me.

"Don't ya use words like that in this house, young lady!" Mrs. Dorsey hollers from her recliner. She sat down in it as soon as Mrs. Alex and I came in, and she hasn't moved since.

"Hi, I'm Sally." The girl speaks so softly I can barely hear her. "I'm sixteen. Nice to meet you, Anna." She runs down the hallway and upstairs like she's running from a dangerous bear. Her black hair is as long as she is. Even though she's older, she's the same height as me and thinner than me. She is like a tiny mouse and sounds like one, too. Sally doesn't look back as she runs toward the stairs.

"I'm not shaking prissy girl's hand. Screw you guys." One girl snorts at Mrs. Alex.

"Patty, you say hi right now. Ya hear me?" Mrs. Dorsey shouts a lot.

A chubby, short girl with pimples and brown hair curled up close to her head turns and puts her middle finger up to Mrs. Alex, just like my older foster brothers used to do to Mother in my first foster home. "Screw you, old lady. I don't have to do shit." She turns to me. "Watch your back, pretty little thing." She mimics picking her nose, and then flips an imaginary booger at me.

A girl with straight, dark hair that falls to her shoulders looks up. "I'm Missy. I'm glad you're here. Bye now." With that, she, too, is gone. Missy is taller than everyone I've seen in this house so far. I bet she is even taller than my Daddy was.

I'm left to stand with the witch-looking woman who's still in her recliner, and of course, Mrs. Alex.

"Anna, take your stuff upstairs. I'm sure the girls will get you settled in." Mrs. Alex points to the stairs.

Really? Two of those girls just told me to watch my back and now I'm going to the wolves by myself.

"Go on, now." Mrs. Dorsey swishes her hands at me.

I have to go. I don't have much of a choice. I never have a choice. My garbage bag hits every step because it's too heavy for me to lift it any higher because it's full of stuff. Now, I'm carrying all my stuff from Sue and Allen's house and now Jessica and Jason's too. Just as my bag clunks the fourth step, I lookup to see how much further I need to go.

Standing at the top of the stairs are Nisa, Patty, and some other girl who wasn't downstairs with all the others—and she doesn't look like she has any hair.

"She *is* fancy. You're right, Nisa."

Nisa giggles and punches the girl in the arm. "I told you, Kelly. She's *fancy*-fancy."

Keep going. Don't show them you're afraid. Keep going. I talk to myself, repeating the same thing again and again 'til I get past the girls. *Never show weakness. Never show weakness. Never show—*

"In here, Anna Snow!" Liz yells out of a doorway. "Your bed's in here."

Even though she yells, I like her friendly voice. I stop as soon as I get in the doorway. I've seen nothing like it. I really want my old room back. I never knew a bedroom could be so big with so many beds in one place. There were five bunk beds lined up on both sides of the room with a small walkway between them.

The rose wallpaper has big pieces ripped off, showing old plaster. The floor is made up of wood boards which looks like the plywood that Jason kept in the barn to do house projects. Except the floor in this room is gross because it has big stains all over it. And all the beds have old torn-up blankets and pillows.

"Anna Snow, down here." I follow her voice to the end of the room by the small, round window. Are we sleeping in the attic? This is a long way from my princess bedroom at Jessica and Jason's.

Keep walking." Liz smiles. "Your bed is with me. You'll sleep on the bottom bunk because I like the top."

I follow her to my bed. Before I sit down, I see it.

A note.

I'm careful not to tear it when I open it. The page is covered in words with small, pretty handwriting.

Welcome, new girl. We're bunk buddies and I hope you don't mind, but I took the top. I am a nice person. I really hope you're Black like me. I get so tired of being the only Black girl here. Everyone picks on me and calls me dirty all the time. Please don't call me dirty. It's just the color of my skin and I hate being called names and treated differently. So, I have my fingers crossed that you're Black like me. Liz.

Chapter 20
Haircut

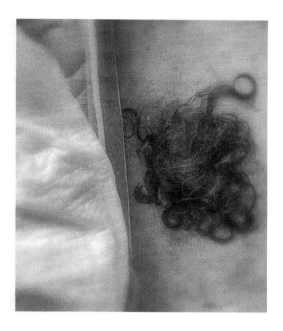

I feel sad for Liz because her skin is pretty, so it's really sad that the other girls don't see that. I wish I was that color. I'm confused, though, because her skin doesn't look black to me, it's more dark brown, like chocolate. So, I shrug my shoulders and stand up to see Liz on the top bunk.

She has a tear on her face. "It's okay, Anna Snow, that you're not Black. I will still be your friend if you like."

I nod then lean in to her so no other girls can hear me. "Can I ask a question? Why do you say you're Black when your skin is dark brown and looks pretty, like chocolate?" I ask.

"Because I'm Black, silly," she giggles.

"Ah, Liz? You look dark brown." I point to her arm.

"Yes, my skin is dark brown, but I come from Black people. So, I'm Black."

I know she's trying to help me understand, but I'm confused. The only other brown person I ever saw was my friend, Deb, at my church.

"Liz?"

"Yeah?"

"What am I called? What are my people?"

"Really, Anna Snow? You don't know what your people are?"

I shake my head.

She giggles. "You're White. You come from White people."

"Eww. I don't like the color white."

Liz giggles again. She puts her arm next to mine. "See? I'm Black and you're White."

"That's not what I see. You're dark brown, and I look red." We both laugh.

"Shut up, you two." Patty, who's sitting on a bed next to Nisa, says, "We're trying to listen to music down here."

"Stay away from those two if you can, Anna Snow. They're mean girls. Once, they threw all my books in the toilet. All I have is my books because all my brothers and sisters are in different foster homes, so I have nobody but my books."

Liz is like me. "You like to read, Liz?"

"Love it, but call me Lizzy. The mean girls here call me Liz and you don't seem like a mean girl, Anna Snow. And don't call me Elizabeth, because that makes me miss my momma." Liz slides her hand down from her top bunk and I grab it. "Though you're not Black but White, I still think we can be friends. Nice to meet you again, Anna Snow. I'm Lizzy." She giggles.

I shake her hand. "Nice to meet you, Lizzy, but I want to be red, not white."

"You can only be what you are. We don't have a choice what color our skins are." Liz puts her head down to her chest.

"Li—"

The loud, clanging bell sounds off downstairs, echoing in the hallway. It sounds like a loud, blow horn. All the girls cover their ears except for Catrina. She skips through the room, coming to stand next to me. Her pants are wet down to her shoes, and she smells like pee.

154

"Time to eat, Anna Snow," says Catrina. "That's the bell to come downstairs." She grabs my hand.

"Thank you, Catrina." I lean close to her ear and whisper. "I think you had an accident in your pants. Why don't you change so the girls don't pick on you and then go ahead and save me a seat. I'll be right down."

Catrina smiles and claps her hands together. "I will. I will."

"That's groovy, Anna Snow," Lizzy says after Catrina leaves. "Just groovy. It's nice you stuck up for Catrina. Let's go."

I follow Lizzy and as soon as I reach the middle of the stairs, I gag as the odor of pee and dog poop hits me in the face. It's coming from the living room where Mrs. Dorsey must still be sitting in her recliner.

"Get your food yourself," she says. "The hotdogs and mac-'n-cheese are in the kitchen. She shouts at me from her recliner, her voice rattling the windows.

Lizzy leads me into a small kitchen with dishes overflowing in the sink. Everyone grabs a hotdog. I see Mean-Girl-Nisa plop a big pile of mac-'n-cheese onto her paper plate. It's so busy in here with so many girls trying to get food all at the same time.

"Here you go, Anna Snow." Lizzy hands me a paper plate and plastic silverware.

I stare at them. I go from fancy dishes to paper plates.

"When you're done eating, throw your stuff in the garbage can. If Mrs. Dorsey sees it lying around, she makes us clean the kitchen and every dish," Liz says, warning me.

This house brings back the same sense of emptiness I've felt for weeks since Curtis was stolen. Now I'm living in my sadness. It's all dark, dirty, and nasty. In this sadness are other girls living in it with me, but Curtis is not around and there are no memories of him here.

I can't put my guard down here. I can't let my sadness take over. I need to be careful. I already have girls who want to hurt me, otherwise they wouldn't have told me to watch my back. I love you, Curtis, and miss you. I'm trying to find the strength to let go of you, even if it's only for now. I have to keep going, so I can come back to you when I'm all grown up.

"Get the hell out of my way." Patty shoves Lizzy into a cabinet, using a word I've never heard before.

"Don't you know you belong in the back of the line?" Nisa calls her the same thing, and it makes Lizzy put her head down.

155

What are they calling her? Why isn't that a nice name? Well, whatever it is, they are *not* gonna get away with it. No one hurts my friend. I walk past the other girls in line.

"Anna Snow, you have to wait your turn," Tori tells me as I walk by her. "You're new, so you're last."

I say nothing. Then I stop behind Nisa and Patty as they scoop mac-'n-cheese from a huge pot on the stove. I wait. Once they both plop their food onto their plates, I send their food flying into their faces.

"Yay! This is fun!" Catrina claps her hands.

"You bitch!" Nisa screams.

Mac-'n-cheese covers her precious hair, and her hotdog flies across the room. Patty didn't get it as bad as Nisa because most of her food falls to the floor. "You're dead mea—"

"Shut up, Patty." Nisa flings a piece of macaroni at me. "We don't want Mrs. Dorsey to hear us in here and make us stay up all night cleaning the kitchen. We'll get her, don't worry." She glares at me as she stands in front of Patty.

I walk back to Lizzy. "Let's get some food." I grab her hand.

Everyone takes their plates upstairs, so I'm guessing that's where we eat. Good, because I don't want to try to eat while smelling the nastiness of the first floor. The food smells bad enough.

"I don't need you to stick up for me because you're White," Lizzy says to me as I sit on my bunk to try to eat. "White girl sticking up for the poor, little, Black girl." She sings the words while standing in front of me.

"What are you talking about? I stick up and fight for my friends. Why does it matter if you're Black? I can't stick up for you because you're Black?"

Lizzy's eyes opened wide in surprise. She gasped.

"Are people from Black people not supposed to stick up for people from White people? That's the stupidest thing I've ever heard. Aren't we all the same people?" I wish Lizzy wasn't mad at me, and I don't know why she is.

"Okay, okay, I get it. I agree with you. Thanks for sticking up for me. Those girls are seriously *mean*. If I swore, I'd say a swear word to show how mean they are." She sets her food down on my bed and crosses her arms.

"You don't swear?" I ask.

"I try not because Jesus doesn't like it." Lizzy wiggles her nose back and forth as she talks.

"Did you just say *Jesus*, Lizzy?"

"Sure did."

I'm finally feeling warm and fuzzy inside since I arrived. "I love Jesus, too. He's my friend."

"Your *friend*? Jesus is your *friend*?" She closes one eye and tilts her head.

"Yes. I met him in his house when I was in my first foster home. I like going to Jesus's house." I don't take a breath because I'm so excited to talk about my friend. "Lizzy?" I put my plate aside and stand up next to her.

"Yeah?" She picks up her plate and takes her last bite of mac-'n-cheese.

"Why did they call you that word?"

She drops her spoon. "Don't ever say that word, you hear me?" She puts her hand over my mouth. "It's a mean word to call someone whose skin is dark. My momma told me that White people used to have Black people as slaves for hundreds of years. The owners of the slaves used to call Black slaves that name. Momma says it means that we're no good."

"You were a slave?" I'm going to cry. Why would White people do that to Lizzy?

"No, silly. My great-great-great grandparents were. They lived in the South and worked on the plantations. They used to get whipped and everything and were made to pick cotton…"

I sit back down and hold my Teddy as I listen to everything Lizzy can tell me about her Black people and the awful slavery.

"So that's why Nisa called you that name? To be mean?" I ask.

"Yes, she's being mean. She told me once she was going to be my owner," Lizzy whispers.

"What?" I say louder than I intended. Everyone in the room stops talking, including the mean girl herself. "You wait here."

I try to stand up, but Lizzy pulls me back down. "I can handle this on my own," she said, her jaw set.

"I hope you'd fight for me if I need your help? Will you?" My voice cracks as I start to talk because for some reason, I feel like I want to cry, and I don't know why.

Lizzy lets go of my hand and nods. "Of course I will. I'm here."

"So, it's okay for you to fight for me because I'm White, but it's not okay for me to fight for you because you're Black?"

Lizzy shrugs. "I guess that does sound kinda stupid."

"No, it sounds *super* stupid. How about we help each other because we're friends and not because of what color we are." I hold up my pinky. "I got your back."

Liz locks her pinky with mine. "I got yours, too."

At this moment, Lizzy becomes my sister. "By the way, your skin is *still* chocolate and not black."

She giggles. "Anna Snow, you look red and not white."

I giggle with her.

"Ah, looky." Nisa pops us beside us, using that nasty word again. "And she's got a little White friend. Maybe they'll kiss, too."

I punch Nisa in the face. I didn't imagine doing it. I didn't wish to do it. I just did it. This time, I actually *do* it.

"Damn! Did you see that?" Tori asks, yelling. "Go, Anna Snow! Get her!"

Nisa's nose is bleeding and her hands fly up to her face as she staggers backwards.

"Call my friend that nasty name again and see what else happens." All I can see is red. It's like the room disappeared.

Patty gives Nisa a towel and Nisa slinks away, glaring at me as she goes.

I jump onto Liz's bed. "Oh crap. I did it again. I didn't mean to, um, stick up for you. I know that makes you mad."

Lizzy's smile almost covers her whole face. "The heck it does. Don't mess with the *Red Chocolates*." She high-fives me.

Before we know it, Mrs. Dorsey yells up the stairs, "Lights out!"

Lizzy sits on the bed, reading me a book.

"Is it really time for bed?" I ask her.

"Yeah, and if we don't hurry up, we'll have crazy chores tomorrow and trust me, you don't want that. Do you want to read to me tomorrow, Anna Snow? We can take turns."

"Ah, no. I'm not a good reader like you. It's hard for me. So, you can read to me, if you like."

"How about I help you read?" Lizzy smiles at me as she closes the worn book.

"Why does your book look so old?"

As Lizzy looks at me with her sad eyes, I felt my heart sink. I haven't known her that long, but I feel like I can trust her.

"It's the only thing I have from living with my birth mother." She wipes a tear. "I don't want to talk about it anymore."

"Okay." I know exactly how she feels. I still don't want to talk about my brother.

"You two shut up and go to bed. We don't want chores tomorrow because of you," Nisa practically hisses at us like the snake she is. She and Patty share a bunk and they're already under their covers.

"Make sure you sleep with your eyes open tonight, Anna Snow," Patty says in a sing-song voice.

"Oooooh," the girls whisper.

I ignore them. "Lizzy?"

"Yeah, Anna Snow?" Lizzy climbs into her bunk.

"First, call me Anna and, next, why don't we brush our teeth?"

The girls around me laugh.

"I like calling you Anna Snow. It's fancy. And we don't brush our teeth here. Now shush and go to sleep. We don't want chores tomorrow."

Chores don't scare me. I'm used to getting up early every morning and feeding my goats. Goats. I sigh, trying to breathe away the pain in my stomach.

Will missing stuff ever get any easier?

***

"Let's go! We have chores to get done today!" Mrs. Dorsey sounds like she's standing in our room. The sunlight shines through the small window and hits me right in the eyes.

The sun always seems so happy. Everything is bright outside. I don't want to feel brightness right now. I'm sad. Can't the Earth let me be sad instead of trying to make the outside world look and feel happy around me? I will be happy someday, just not right now. I have a feeling that I will have to fight to make it here.

Hey Curtis. I miss you and hope you are doing okay in your new home.

I move my doll and Curtis's Teddy against the wall and sit up. Then, I see it. There's a big blob of hair on the floor by my bed. Nisa and Patty are up already, leaning against the bunk next to mine, staring at me.

159

Lizzy jumps down from her bunk above me and gasps.

My first morning in this new hell and all the girls are staring at me?

"Hello, fancy girl. How's your hair this morning?"

Why would Lisa ask ab—

My hands fly up to my head as I look at the hair on the floor.

Spikes. All I feel are spikes where my hair's supposed to be. I went to bed in a ponytail—it's gone.

"Noooooooooooo!" I jump out of bed. "Who did this? Who did this to my hair?"

Chapter 21
Circle of Sisters

I glare at all of them. "I'm gonna pound the person who did this to me."

Lizzy jumps off her bed. "Anna, calm down. If Mrs. Dorsey hears you, we'll have to do chores all day." Her voice is quiet.

"I don't c—"

The bedroom door flings open. "What the hell is goin' on in here?" Mrs. Dorsey stands in the doorway in her robe, with a cigarette hanging out of her mouth.

"Nothing's going on in here. Nisa fixes her eyes on me and puts her arm out to point. "The new girl fell outta her bed."

"No, I didn't. She cut my hair off while I was sleeping." I point back at Nisa.

"No. I didn't. You don't know who did that. You didn't see me do it, did ya?"

My hand curls into a fist. I jump on Nisa and we both slam to the ground.

I end up sitting on her stomach, so I punch her in the face. That'll show her. *You*—punch—*don't*—punch—*mess*—punch—*with*—punch—*me*—punch.

"Get her! Get her!" some of the girls scream, but no one jumps in to pull me off of her.

Good.

I punch her again. I have had just about *enough* of people making my life awful.

"Git off her, ye young lady! Now!"

I don't care what Mrs. Dorsey says and I land another punch. Nisa's nose bleeds. Good. Cut off my hair, will you?

"Git off her!" Mrs. Dorsey grips my arm and tugs while she screams at me. "Kelly, git 'er off that girl!"

Someone grabs me and pulls while I'm still swinging. Just one more punch. That's all I want. That'll teach her to mess with me.

"Knock it off, kid." Tori says after Kelly sets me on my feet. "I think she got the message." I hear Tori's deep voice, who stands next to me.

I catch my breath. Then, everything in the room goes gray…

"Wow. You should see Nisa's face. I don't think she'll mess with you again," Lizzy whispers to me as I wake up.

Oh, man. I passed out, the first time it's happened here. Now they're all going to make fun of me again. Well, maybe not. I smile.

"Is she all right or not?" Mrs. Dorsey asks.

My eyes focus and I see Lizzy's face above mine.

"You scared the crap out of us," she pats my shoulder.

I hope she means that I scared the crap out of Nisa and her gang of mean girls with my punching, but I'm betting she means about passing out. Maybe both. Both wouldn't be bad. At least they'd learn to stay away from me. I am not a wussy and will stick up for myself if I have to. It's just me in this world and if I can't do it, who will? It's nice to know that I have Lizzy to help me here. But, I'm sure I won't live here forever, or at least, I hope not.

"What is wrong with ya, kid?" Mrs. Dorsey shoves Lizzy aside and stands by the bed that I'm somehow lying on.

"I passed out, that's what happened. It's what happens when I get upset or mad." I don't think I was out long, but someone did put me on this bed and I don't remember it. I don't remember anything that happens when I pass out and it's kinda creepy.

I don't want to be here anymore.

I don't want to be in this disgusting place.

Mrs. Dorsey's cigarette hangs from her mouth with a long bunch of ash on the end—just one more disgusting thing about this place.

"Yeah, well, it don't matter. Y'all are still gonna be doin' chores all day because 'o this crap. Anna Snow, you're gonna start with cleaning da toilets with a toothbrush." She grins a disgusting grin—just like her disgusting cigarette and her disgusting dinner and her whole disgusting house.

I jump off the bed in front of her. "I'm not doing that!" I'm beyond caring about what happens to me. "Nisa cut my hair!" I put my hands on my hips. "Don't you see it, or are you blind?"

Everyone sucks in a big breath and there's not another sound.

Mrs. Dorsey takes a step closer and glares at me. "Ya wanna talk to me dat way, lady?"

"Yup. I do." I take a step closer, too.

Smack.

I fall to the ground, holding my face. Mrs. Dorsey struck me so hard I see spots flying around along with the walls. The spinning room slows. I jump back up and take another step towards her again.

"Are ya doin' da toilets now?" she asks.

"Nope. I'm not doin' ya toilet." I mock how she talks.

Smack.

This time, I didn't fall down because I knew it was coming. Instead, I turn my head back around and face her. She throws her cigarette on the floor and puts it out with her foot.

"How 'bout now?" She glares at me and presses her lips together. Good. I don't want to look at her disgusting teeth.

"Nope. I'm not doin' ya toilet. Do you have a hard time hearing me, or do you just have a hard time talking?"

Bam.

I fall to the floor, and blood flies out of my nose and drips on the plywood beneath me, turning it brown. Lizzy jumps between me and Mrs. Dorsey. I can tell it's her by her feet, because they're chocolate.

"Stay down and agree to do the toilet, Anna Snow!"

I wipe the blood with my arm and I stand up—slower this time because the room spins.

Everyone's staring at me with wide eyes as I take two steps to stand

163

in front of Mrs. Dorsey again. "I'm not going to clean your disgusting toilets with a toothbrush. You can hit me as much as you want. Get your lazy ass off your chair and clean this disgusting house yourself."

Bam.

"Anna Snow, are you okay? Anna Snow?"

I hear Lizzy. My eyes open again. I'm on the floor with my face in a pile of blood. "Stop it, Anna. Don't fight her. You won't win." She hisses the words at me.

It's hard for me to stand up, but I do so, slowly and carefully.

Mrs. Dorsey is still standing there, but, this time, with a belt in her hand.

I step in front of her, rocking back and forth as I try to stay on my feet. I taste the blood as it runs into my mouth. One of my eyes throbs, making Mrs. Dorsey looks bigger, yet smaller somehow.

"Well? Are ya gonna clean da toilets?" She smacks the belt against the palm of her hand just like Derek used to do in my first foster home when we played the Book Game.

I squeeze my eyes shut. Mrs. Dorsey is gone, and now Derek is standing in front of me. *How did he find me here? Does he know Mrs. Dorsey?*

Each time Derek smacks his hand with the belt, my eyes squeeze shut. I have no control over them.

"Are you gonna drop those books? Are you gonna drop them now?" I know what Derek will do if I don't drop them. He'll beat me with the belt, like all the times before.

I stare at his fat face. "No, I'm not going to," I scream.

The first hit of the belt cuts into the skin on my arms.

Screams erupt around me. "Stop it! Stop it! You're going to kill her!"

My skin on my legs splits open with each hit after that. And then the room gets fuzzy…

My eyes jolt open when a cold cloth touches my face.

"Don't move, Anna Snow."

I open my eyes and see Lizzy, as well as Tori, Sally, Patty, Missy, Kelly, and Catrina around my bed. Then I see—

Nisa.

"*Derek?*" I scream.

Lizzy presses the cloth against my face again and pushes me down on the bed. "Lay down. You're hurt. Who's Derek? There's no one here with that name."

My right arm feels like someone ripped it off. I reach over to grab it.

"Don't touch it. It's still bleeding," Lizzy sounds serious.

"Derek wasn't here?" I ask in a whisper. I swear I saw him standing with the belt in his hands. "Didn't you see Derek hit me with the belt?"

"That was Mrs. Dorsey," Missy whispers loudly, moving closer to my bed.

"Mrs. Dorsey?" I feel like everyone and everything is fading again.

And then Nisa comes up to my bed. "Anna, I'm sorry. I'm the one who cut your hair, but you knocked my socks off. I'm sorry Mrs. Dorsey did that to you. No matter what our fights are, we have to stick together."

"Yeah. Damn straight," Patty says. "We can fight each other if we want to, but nobody better mess with any of us." I remember the conversation I had with Curtis about other foster kids. We didn't know if there were any others, and now a circle of them are standing around me.

Tori steps up next to her. "I gotta say, you're one badass chick—for a runt, that is." She holds her hand up.

It takes me a second, but I smack it. "And, by the way, short hair on you looks badass." She smiles and sits down at the end of my bed.

"I can fix that, Anna," Nisa says. "I used to watch my mom cut hair before the drugs made them take us away from her. So, I can fix that for you." A tear slides down the bump on her face—the one I gave her.

"By the way," Sally says, her voice squeaking. "Lizzy cleaned your toilets. That's the only way we could get Mrs. Dorsey to stop hitting you with the belt."

I look at my new best friend. She stuck up for me. Maybe I'm not all alone in this world after all. "Um… Lizzy? How did you have time to clean the toilets?"

"Girl, you were out for a few hours. You'd wake up and go back to sleep. We all took turns staying with you to make sure you were okay." Lizzy's eyes moved around to all the girls standing by my bed.

"I nnnneeevverrrr llllllleft you. IIIIII stayyyyyeeed the wwwwwhooooole timmmme." Catrina smiles as she tells me what she did for me.

"Thank you, Catrina."

I have friends. These girls are watching out for me.

"Last darn time I'll clean the toilet for you." Lizzy crosses her arms. "So please don't pick another fight with Mrs. Dorsey, no matter how much you want to."

Everyone laughs nervously.

Though every part of my body hurts, for a change, my heart does not. I have a family of sisters, and nobody better mess with them or me.

I stayed in bed all day and I didn't eat or drink anything, and, thankfully Mrs. Dorsey leaves me alone.

I sleep here and there, but mostly think about Curtis and even Jessica and Jason, the goats, Dottie, Thunder, and Daddy. If only I could close my eyes and wish myself back to the barn with my friends... I would. This place is awful. I squeeze my eyes tighter together, thinking this might make my wish come true. But like many things, this is real. I can't wish my brother back, just like I can't wish to be back with Jess and Jason.

I hear footsteps as someone comes into the room. For a moment, I hope it's one of them, but then reality smacks me in the face harder than Mrs. Dorsey ever could.

"I want to give it to her!" Catrina's voice carries from the door all the way to my bed.

The girls seem friendlier to her now. "Okay, but don't drool on it," Nisa says, obviously irritated but calm.

"We brought you a hotdog and mac-'n-cheese." Catrina is so happy she almost drops it all over me.

"Yeah, that bitch said you could go hungry, so we decided to give you some of ours." Patty looks proud with her head held high.

That explains why there are so many pieces of hotdogs all over my plate. "Thanks, guys." I sit up.

"Oh boy." Lizzy lets out a big breath. "Whatever you do, don't look in the mirror. Your face looks all black and blue—just like both of your eyes."

"I think you look badass, Anna Snow," Tori says. "Like a ninja or something."

"Sit in this chair." Nisa holds up a pair of scissors. "Let's fix your hair."

I set my plate aside and stand. I hurt all over—like I've been run over by a train.

"Easy. Go slow." Lizzy holds my hand as I walk to the chair.

166

Everyone is around us and I know—right now, at this moment—that I'm not alone. These girls will protect me. I can feel it. And... I them. I look at Nisa holding the scissors and make a decision to trust her, even though she's the reason my hair needs to be fixed. She's the hardest to trust, but I'm going to do it, anyway.

Sally holds a mirror up in front of my face. "See? You look pretty."

I cringe when I see what I look like. The girls weren't exaggerating. Mrs. Dorsey beat me good.

"If I could, I would do something to fix those teeth for you, so people won't pick on you. Someday, see a dentist and ask him to make your teeth straight," Nisa says.

I realized not one of the girls had called me a buck-tooth beaver here. I'm called that name wherever I go.

"Hell no. They give you needles. I'd stay away from the dentist if I were you. I'd rather have beaver teeth than a needle being shoved in my mouth. Uh uh. Ahh. No, thank you." Patty folds her hands and walks to her bunk. From the other side of the room, she says, "No dentist for me, ever."

I'll take the needle in the mouth to have straight, pretty teeth. I must remember that when I get old. I have to get Curtis and visit a dentist.

I look in the mirror in front of me. This is the first time I've seen myself since I've lived here. There are no mirrors anywhere, and I can't remember the last time I showered or brushed my teeth. I don't recognize this girl. She is not the clean, pretty, dressed up thing that rode in the yellow Corvette with Jess. I want to cry.

"Huh? What do you think?" Nisa's voice brings me out of my memories of Jess.

"It looks nice, Nisa. Thank you."

Sally holds the mirror up a little longer. Now, my unibrow and buck teeth *really* stand out. My friends are trying to be nice. I look really ugly. My eyes are so swollen I wonder how I can see out of them.

"I'm sorry, Anna," Nisa mumbles as she walks past me and puts the scissors under her pillow.

I turn to Lizzy. "Why does she keep those under her pillow?"

"Because she cuts herself when she's upset."

"She *what*? My voice cracks as it rises in pitch.

Nisa walks back and sits with the rest of the girls on the floor. Lizzy and I go back to sitting on our bottom bunk.

"I cut when I'm upset." Nisa shrugs. "Because I don't want my heart to hurt, I'd rather make my body hurt instead."

Everyone's eyes are enormous, and their mouths are open. No one says anything. I can't believe Nisa told us all something so personal.

"Come on, you guys. I know you've all seen me do it over the past months." She looks around the circle, then pulls up her sleeves and shorts to show us her scars.

Patty and Kelly nod. Are they agreeing with Nisa? Did they see her cut herself before?

"Do you still feel sad later when your cut doesn't hurt anymore?" I have to know, though cutting myself sounds scary. I wish I could find a way to make all my sadness go away.

"Yeah. That's why I haven't done it over the last few weeks. Because it doesn't change anything. I'm still sad about being a kid no one wants." Nisa puts her head down.

"I'm tired of pretending I'm a girl." Tori joins the conversation.

"Ah, Tori? I've seen you naked. You're a girl." Kelly giggles.

"No, dummy. I know I'm a *girl*, but everyone calls me a boy, so I started dressing like one."

"So, that's why you dress like a boy and keep your hair short?" Nisa asks.

"Yeah. Tori's voice cracks as she speaks, "It's hard, getting picked on and being a foster kid on top of it, you know."

"Actually, we don't, Tori." Nisa speaks up again.

Tori wipes the tear on her cheek. "Everyone thinks we're rejects. Including people at school. Kids have picked on me for not having a mom and dad for as long as I can remember. I hated father and daughter day. I hated the father and daughter dance. I hated it all. So, I began to act up so I could get kicked out of school when those things were happening. That way, I always had an excuse of why I couldn't go rather than telling people it's because I don't have a father. Foster homes don't want us. How can they if our own parents didn't want us? I'm here because they can't find a foster home who will take me. Mrs. Alex told me if I don't make it here, I'm heading to jail for kids."

My heart hurts for Tori. So far, she's been really nice to me. Why would she have to go to jail? It's not her fault no one wants her. Wait… no one seems to want me either.

"Plus, I'm tired of pretending to be someone I'm not." Why do I have to dress like a girl because I'm a girl? I'm okay looking and dressing like a boy.

"If you don't say anything, you can pass for a boy," Sally whispers.

"I have anxiety so bad that I'm afraid of everything. My mind makes up things for me to be afraid of. Every night, I go to sleep worrying that this house is going to catch on fire from Mrs. Dorsey's cigarette falling out of her mouth." Sally is shaking just talking about it.

"Sally, if there's a fire, we can all tie our sheets together and we can climb down the window," I point to the window in our bedroom.

That's a brilliant plan! What gave you the idea to do that?" Sally leans her head further in the circle to see me.

"It's something that my last foster family told me to do if there was ever a fire." Sadness tugs at me as I remember Jess showing me how to do that.

Sally stops talking. But, that's the most I've heard her say since I moved in.

"Do you guys have any idea how hard it is to be the only Black girl living with all White people?" Lizzy slides down from my bed to join the circle of girls on the floor. "I always feel different and people always stare at me when I go someplace with my White foster parents. I hate that. I hate the stare." Lizzy sounds sad.

"Your brown skin is beautiful and I'm jealous," Nisa says. "I think that's why I always pick on you. You're always tan. I wish I could look like that. I noticed that when I'm jealous of people, I tend to be mean to them. Just like you, Anna. You walked in here all fancy in your pretty clothes, and I hated and wanted to hurt you. But we are all the same no matter where we come from. Because the reality is—we come from nowhere."

I decide to slide off the bed to sit next to Lizzy on the floor. "Ouch."

"Join our circle time, Anna Snow." Kelly claps her hands.

"Who else wants to share a dark secret?"

Tori puts her hands up. One by one, we grab each other's hands. Patty is the last one to grab Nisa's hand before she speaks. I look around for Catrina and noticed that she must've gone back to her bed to play by herself.

"Wait. Catrina, come here," Nisa yells toward Catrina's bed, where the girl is playing with a tall, skinny doll.

She walks over to us skipping and acting goofy, clapping her hands together but making no noise.

169

"Catrina, come sit by Lizzy and me."

" I move away from Lizzy so that Catrina has room to sit between us. The other girls try to be nice to her, but it's hard for them because Catrina is annoying. Or at least that is what I've seen since yesterday. She never stops moving. Even sitting with us now, my hand is in constant motion locked with hers.

"We're foster sisters. We'll stick up for one another." Nisa stops talking and looks around the room.

Patty speaks first. "Agreed."

Kelly sits holding her hand. "Agreed."

Then Missy. "Agreed."

Sally whispers, "Agreed."

Lori looks like she's crying. "I've always felt like I don't fit in with girls because girls make fun of me. This is the first time I found a bunch of cool bitches. So, hell yeah, agreed."

"I agree with Lori. I always feel like everyone hates me because I'm Black. This is super groovy. But as my sisters, can you please stop saying that nasty word. I hate it." Lizzy holds her head up, but her chin is quivering like she's about to cry.

At the same time, both Nisa and Patty speak. "Sorry."

Lizzy smiles. "Agreed."

"I agree. I agree." Catrina lets go of our hands so she can clap in front of her.

"Okay, Catrina." Nisa's voice is kind, and this makes me smile. It's so different from just a few hours ago.

I grab Catrina's hand again and so does Lizzy. I feel the volcano coming. I am not the only foster child. I am not alone and other foster kids feel the same way I do. Holy crap, I'm going to cry in front of these girls. I feel the lump in my throat. I can't stop it, and I can't leave this group. I don't want them to get mad at me.

Stop it, Anna. Stop it.

A single tear slides down my cheek. Everyone is quiet, waiting for me to talk. "I just lost my brother before I came here. They ripped him out of my arms at my last foster home. That horrible witch, Mrs. Alex, did it. He was all I had left in this world." The rest of my tears want to escape, but I'm not going to let that happen. I find a little control to hold them back. "I felt alone." I pause again to swallow to hold the lump in place.

A few of the girls look at each other while waiting for me to continue.

I sink my head into my chest. "That is, 'til now. With all of you, I know that I'm not the only foster kid. That all those of us in this group know what it's like to be us. No one else will ever know what it's like. What it's like to be ripped out of families' homes again and again. What it's like to go to a new place with strangers. What it's like to be garbage and carry it with you everywhere. What it's like to know that no one wants you. What it's like to be… us."

I look up and around the circle. Everyone has tears on their faces, but Catrina is smiling.

Nisa lays back on the floor with her arms in the air. We all watch for a second. Then one by one we each do it. Our shoulders make a perfect circle with our hands in the air.

"No one understands us, but foster kids will *always* get it. Even if we don't know each other, once we know that someone's a foster kid, they become our brothers and sisters because—we know." Nisa sounds like she's speaking in front of a group of people. I can't see her. All I can see is all our hands in the air.

"We are a circle of sisters." Tori's voice crackles.

Chapter 22
Wolf Pack

"Foster kids are a wolf pack. Like the movie I watched at my last home. Wolves stick together and take care of each other," Kelly says.

"Yes, we are. From this night forward, we all make a pact that we agree to always help another foster child, no matter who they are. We are a foster care wolf pack. The only people who will ever understand how we had to live our lives are other foster kids. So, we always protect them and watch out for them and each other. Deal?"

"We're a pack and will always protect others." Nisa sings the words in a quiet voice.

"We're a pack and will always protect others like us." Tori changes it up a little, and we all follow.

As the circle breaks up, I sit on my bed and look at my dinner plate. I slide it under the bed so the witch won't find it and punish us with chores.

I lie in my bed, turn toward the wall, and hug my Raggedy and Teddy. My entire body hurts, but for the first time in a long time, my heart feels a little lighter because I don't feel like I'm all alone anymore.

Thank you, Jesus, for bringing me sisters. I know you are trying to help me, so I won't feel alone while you try to help my brother stop killing animals. I know he doesn't talk to you, but maybe, someday, he will. But can you talk to him and tell him I love and miss him? Tell him I will come to get him soon. Also, can you help my face, arms, and legs stop hurting from Mrs. Dorsey beating me? Maybe you should help Mrs. Dorsey, too, because she is one mean lady. Well, I'm tired and going to sleep. Goodnight, Jesus.

***

"Get off her!" I lunge at Mrs. Dorsey. Catrina's cries ring through my head with each lash.

"Ya dumb girl. Why piss ya self in the living room?" Mrs. Dorsey swings the belt again.

Nisa shoves Catrina out of the way, while Tori and Kelly tackle Mrs. Dorsey.

"Aaahh!" Mrs. Dorsey cries out when she hits the floor.

"Stop hitting her, you old bitch! How would you like us to hit you the way you're hitting Catrina?" Tori screams at her.

"Okay, okay!" Mrs. Dorsey swings her arms, trying to get Tori off her.

"You're going to stop hitting Catrina, right? Tori asks.

"Get off me you ungrateful bitches," Mrs. Dorsey hollers.

Mrs. Dorsey climbs to her knees and then to her feet. She stands in front of us, glaring.

I step forward. "You can't keep hitting us like you do. It's not okay—"

"Come on, Anna Snow."

Someone shakes my shoulders.

"Wake up."

My eyes flutter as I try to open them—but they won't open.

I feel my face—it stings and there's warm blood everywhere—again. My front teeth hurt. I cry out.

"Don't move. We saw a tooth go flying. We think Mrs. Dorsey knocked your teeth out," Sally whispers close to my ear.

"Get her cleaned up and all of you can go to bed without dinner. You have school tomorrow," she says, her voice vile and loud.

Wait. Did she say *school*?

I sit up and feel my mouth. One of my front teeth is broken in half. Blood drips from my nose, so Lizzy gives me a sock to use. "What the heck happened?" I ask Lizzy.

"Mrs. Dorsey punched you in the face and knocked you out. She then ran to our bedroom door, and she shut it so we didn't chase after her.

"Ouch, she got me good." My face is still a little bruised from her hitting me last week, and my tooth really hurts.

"Stop touching them, silly." Silly is Lizzy's favorite word.

As I sit on the floor, so do my sisters. Patty takes care of the cuts on Catrina's face and arms, while Lizzy takes care of me.

"So, we really have school tomorrow?" I ask.

"Yeah, we do. I'm not happy about going into tenth grade."

"I'm with you." Tori high fives Nisa.

"You know we can't act like we're friends in school, right?" Tori says. "My friends will think I've lost my mind being friends with a cheerleader. That cannot happen. But if you need anything, Nisa, you let me know and I've got your back." Tori gives her a thumbs-up.

"I agree. The rest of the cheerleaders won't get it either. But know that I'll stick up for you no matter where we are or who's around. Wolf pack." Nisa puts her hand in a fist and hits it against Tori's shoulder.

"The one thing I hate about school is the bus ride. Kids always pick on me about my teeth," I say, gingerly touching my broken tooth. It'll be even worse now.

"Don't worry, Anna Snow, you can sit with me." Lizzy taps my shoulder.

"We can all sit together or separate, but let's sit one seat apart." Patty points to all of us sitting on the floor. "That way, we know if someone is giving any of us crap."

"Why don't we go to bed? It's dark and we're not getting dinner, anyway." Nisa waves her hand in the air.

I agree with Nisa. I throw away the gross sock soaked in my blood, and climb into bed with Teddy and my doll, Raggedy.

***

174

The bell rings, signaling for us to walk into the school. The bus ride was good as I sat with Lizzy. The rest of the girls sat in separate seats. Catrina sat with Sally.

"This school is so much bigger than my other one."

Lizzy squeezes my hand for a second. "You got this. If you can punch out Nisa and take Mrs. Dorsey's punch, you can do this school. I wish I could fight like you." Lizzy walks slower.

I turn to her. "I wish I was smart like you."

"You're smarter than you think, Anna Snow. Please don't be nervous. I'll walk you inside to the office before I head over to my school."

We walk in the door, and a teacher steps in front of us. "Are you..." The teacher stops talking and stares at me. She tilts her head at first and then moves it side-to-side as she looks at me. "Are you Anna Snow?"

"Um... yeah?"

"Sweetie, come with me so we can get you registered." Mrs. Strudder called this morning and said she forgot to do it and that you're going into third grade."

"Mrs. Strudder?" I ask.

"Yes, that is your foster mother's last name." The teacher tells me as she leans closer to my face.

Weird. I wonder why we call her Mrs. Dorsey. I shrug in my head because I don't really care why we call her what we do. But I do care that she's trying to put me in a lower grade.

"That's a lie. She's a liar. I'm going to be in fifth grade. I finished fourth grade at my old school."

The teacher tilts her head to the side. "Okay, come with me and let's see what we can find out."

"Bye, Lizzy."

"Bye, Anna. I'll see you tonight on the bus."

"You best be getting to the middle school, Elizabeth. Good luck in eighth grade."

This teacher acts like she already knows Lizzy. I'll have to ask Lizzy about it tonight at the house. We go in separate directions, and I follow the teacher. She asks me to sit in the chair while she talks to the principal.

I pick at my fingernails while waiting. My broken tooth throbs. I reach up and feel that my eye is still swollen and puffy. It still hurts to touch it.

175

"Anna Snow. Hello. I'm the principal here, Mr. Doyle. Please follow me."

I follow the tall man into his office.

"Take a chair."

I sit in one of the two chairs in front of his desk.

"I want to ask you a few questions. Is that okay? Can we get you all set up for school?"

I slide to the edge of my seat. "I'm supposed to be in fifth grade. That means Mrs. Dorsey doesn't know what she's talking about. Please don't put me in third grade. You can call m—"

"It's okay, Anna." Mr. Doyle holds his hand in the air. "I know you're supposed to be in fifth grade. I have some other questions."

Mr. Doyle doesn't ask the other questions, though. He just keeps staring at me and doesn't say anything. I play with my fingers because it gives me something to do while I wait. I don't like silences so I need something or I'll go nuts, and that will cause other problems I don't need.

He takes a big breath, shakes his head, and then lets it out. "What happened to your face?"

My hands move to my black-and-blue eyes and the bump on my cheek. I don't know what to say. Actually, I do, but what good is it going to do for me to tell him all about Mrs. Dorsey being abusive? It won't change anything.

Mr. Doyle speaks again. "Yes, that's my point. Your face looks like it would hurt. I know all the girls who live in that foster home, and I'm going to call each one in and find out who did that to you. We're going to start with Tori Rhimes. She has a history of trouble."

"But Tori didn't do this. She's my friend."

Mr. Doyle raises an eyebrow, but doesn't say anything.

"I mean it. Tori didn't do this."

Mr. Doyle sighs. "She has a history of getting into fights, so we may need to find her a new place to live. She attacked a girl in a foster home before. I can call her caseworker to come move her so you can be safe." He acts like he cares about me, but he doesn't listen to me.

"You're not listening to me." My voice goes louder.

"It may be time for Tori to be moved to juvie."

"What's juvie?" I ask.

"It's a secure facility for teens who are troublemakers."

"Tori's not a troublemaker. She's my friend." My loud voice booms throughout his office.

I jump as Tori comes barging through the door.

"Anna Snow, are you okay? I thought I heard you. Don't tell him anything. Don't tell him." Tori stands behind my chair.

"Hello, Tori. I'm glad you joined us. There's a lot going on this morning. I think it's time for a higher level of care for you, so I'm calling your caseworker." Mr. Doyle whispers, but his words are stern.

Tori turns as white as a ghost and her eyes get big. She acts tough all the time, so I've never seen this look on her face before. "I didn't touch Anna. This is not my work." She sounds like she is begging him to believe her.

My neck hurts, as I have to keep turning around to see her standing behind me. When Mr. Doyle looks in his desk for something, Tori and I look at each other. She shakes her head at me.

I squeeze my hands together as I watch him pick up his phone and dial a number. I won't let her take the blame for Mrs. Dorsey, I won't. I have to protect Tori.

I turn around and Tori moves to my side. "Tori?"

She looks down at me.

"Wolf pack," I whisper.

I whip my head around, determined to set things right. "Tori didn't do it to me." I say loudly. "Mr. Doyle, Mrs. *Dorsey* did it."

Mr. Doyle stops dialing, stares at me for a minute, then hangs the phone up.

I stand up and grab Tori's hand.

"Wolf pack," she whispers.

"Ms. Rhimes, is this the truth?"

We let go of each other's hands.

Tori puts her head down, and with a deep voice, she responds to Mr. Doyle. "Yeah. Mrs. Dorsey did that to her face. She even broke her tooth."

Phew. Now Tori won't have to move to a juvie. We can go home and call it good.

"Okay, Ms. Rhimes. You can head back to the high school and thank you for coming in. Ask one of the secretaries for a pass."

"Bye, Anna Snow." She high-fives me.

"Ms. Snow, can you sit back down, please? I need to speak with the staff for a minute." He walks out of the office.

I stay in the fancy chair in front of his desk while I wait. I can't wait to see my foster sisters tonight. I enjoy knowing I have them if I ever need them for anything. I'm so glad I told him about Mrs. Dorsey because Tori won't have to move. We protected each other because we're a wolf pack.

A woman with a kind smile taps on the door and then enters. "Anna? I'm Ms. Shirley. I'm going to take you for a walk and show you around while we wait for Mr. Doyle." She stops mid-step for a second and a look comes over her.

I could tell by the way she looked at me that she had noticed my messed-up face.

She looks nice enough, though. "Sure," I say, standing up.

I follow her around the school where she shows me all the places I need to know. I look into the windows of the classrooms as we walk past them, wondering which one will be mine. My stomach hurts a little thinking about making new school friends, but I know now that I'm not totally alone. I wonder if Curtis is in school now too, somewhere. Is he okay?

After we walk around the entire school, she returns me to the principal's office and tells me to sit tight until he gets back.

Mr. Doyle walks around his desk and sits down. "Ms. Anna, as a principal, my job is to make sure that all my students are safe and that I do my part to protect them. So, please understand why I had to do what I just did." He pauses. "I called your caseworker, and she's out in the waiting area. She needs to take you to another foster home. You can't go back to Mrs. Dorsey's because she's going to be investigated for child abuse."

I'm a large ice cube. I can't move. I can't hear what Mr. Doyle is saying anymore. Did I hear him right? Did he just say he called my caseworker? Did he just tell me that I have to move to *another* foster home and *leave* my foster sisters? Did he? Did he?

I try to get up, but my legs refuse to move.

Anna, get up! You have to run away! Get up!

My legs don't listen. I can't move them.

I can't leave these girls. This is the first time I feel like someone other than Curtis cares for me. Why did I have to come to school today? Why did Mrs. Dorsey send me? She had to have known people would want to know. It's all her fault. Why is it everyone else's fault, but I'm the one that has to move?

178

I empty all the air I have in my lungs. My hands sweat and my heart pounds so hard it hurts my chest. My ears and my head feel as if they're on fire.

Then, I hear her behind me.

Mrs. Alex.

"Anna Snow, it's time to go." Mrs. Alex's voice sounds as cold as it always does.

I stand. "Bye Mr. Doyle." With that, I walk out of the school, saying nothing to anyone else.

I stand by Mrs. Alex's green car. Is she going to take me to get my stuff? I want to see the girls, but I don't want to see Mrs. Dorsey.

"No need to stand there Anna, get in the car."

I open the door and I see that my garbage bag, Teddy and Raggedy, are already in the back seat waiting for me. I look up at Mrs. Alex and see her witchy eyes staring at my broken face.

Is she going to ask me about it? I don't move, so I can think of a lie to tell her when she asks me how it happened.

"I got everything for you already. You won't be going back to Mrs. Dorsey's."

That's it? That's all she's going to say to me? She's not going to ask me what happened to my face?

The engine starts.

Nope, this mean lady doesn't even ask. I always thought that she didn't care about Curtis and me, but this proves it. I open the car door and scooch over my garbage bag so I can sit behind Mrs. Alex. I don't want to look at her.

"What about all the other girls?" I ask.

"They are moving as well. You are all going to separate places."

Sadness has broken my heart again. Here I go once more, saying *just another goodbye*…

…Not just to people, but—my sisters.

Goodbye Nisa.

Goodbye Missy.

Goodbye Tori.

Goodbye Kelly.

Goodbye Catrina.

Goodbye Patty.

Goodbye Sally.

And... goodbye to my best friend—Lizzy.

I lean my head against the window and allow my tears to escape. I hope this lets the pain out that I have inside my gut.

A tear makes it's way down my cheek as I say goodbye to another world that will soon be dead to me.

Will I ever find someone who wants me?

Will I ever find someone to love me?

Will I ever stop being garbage and thrown away trash?

Though I can not answer any of those questions. What I do know is that this car...

Is taking me to yet another world where I have no idea what can happen to me.

ABOUT THE AUTHOR

Dr. Sharon Zaffarese-Dippold's writing comes from her own lived experiences as a child who exper-ienced multiple foster care and family placement moves involving all forms of childhood abuse and trauma.

Dr. Dippold attended approximately ten or more schools during her formative years as she moved from place to place. In spite of that, she earned a Bachelor in Social Work, a Masters in Social Work, and earned her PhD in Human Services from Capella University with a concentration in Human Behavior/Counseling Studies.

Her Doctoral Dissertation was published in 2016, The Lived Experience Of Former Foster Children Who Had to Move Their Belongings In Garbage Bags. A public speaker and trainer on foster care topics related to her story, her experience with bullying led her to create "INAM- It's Not About Me," an anti-bullying program that she presents in the school systems to deflect the impact of being bullied on children.

Dr. Zaffarese-Dippold lives in Saint Mary's, Pennsylvania, with her husband, where she enjoys spending time with her children and grandchildren. She has been recognized for donating 10% of all net proceeds from her first book "Just Another Slice," to the Organization "Together We Rise," which helps foster children to be moved with dignity by replacing garbage bags with duffel bags.

JUST another HIDING PLACE

A Foster Care Story
Based on True Events.

DR. SHARON ZAFFARESE-DIPPOLD

Garbage Bag Life 4

Just Another Hiding Place

How do you hide from the monsters in your own house?

Anna Snow, caught in the foster care merry-go-round, is still being shuffled from house to house, but none of them are ever really home. By the time she's ten years old, she's been moved nine times, three of them happening in under three months. Anna finds a measure of love in one home, but the system yanks her away, simply because her caring foster mother is Black.

Anna's also still dealing with the ache of being separated from her brother. Her only connection to him is the teddy bear he dropped as he was ripped from her arms. She'll never see her brother again, but she clings to the bear, along with her treasured Raggedy Doll, reminding her she is not alone through each wrenching move. In each foster home she finds a place to hide from those hurting her, but she'll soon discover she'll need to find hiding spots again to escape a far more horrific kind of abuse.

In this fourth book in the "Garbage Bag Life" series, Anna is forced to face unimaginable loss and the dangers to a young girl growing up in a system rife with groomers and abusers.

Editor(s)/Artistic Creator Bios

Judi Fennell is a #1 Best-Selling Amazon author, an award-winning author, and the recipient of *Publishers Weekly* starred reviews, with over twenty titles to her name domestically and internationally. She has been helping other authors realize their dream of publication for over a decade, and counts authors at all levels of their career as her clients, from "newbies" to NYT best-sellers, along with several hybrid publishers. You can find her books at www.JudiFennell.com and get help with your writing journey—from editing to cover design to formatting, and consultation—at www.formatting4U.com.

Amy Mullen (Editor)—is a freelance writer, editor, and romance author living in Corning, NY with her family and her pets. Besides writing, Amy enjoys feeding the critters in her backyard, reading, and rooting for the Buffalo Bills, but not necessarily in that order. She is the author of *A Stormy Knight, Redefining Rayne*, and *Her Darkest Knight*.

Acknowledgments

Judi Fennell (formatting4u.com)—Thank you for your beautiful cover creation, professional guidance, support, and top-notch professional editing. You provide instructions for each step in the publishing process. You are the whole package. Further, I am excited for you to be the voice of Sarah and, in this book, Anna in the audiobooks.

Amy Mullen (Editor) of Corning, New York—Thank you for your editorial assistance. You started this process with me twenty years ago. I'm excited to have you once again on this journey.

Kate Sheridan (blurbwriter.com)—Thank you for the beautifully written back cover. It is a powerful synopsis of the book.

My Family—Thank you for all your continued support and guidance. Without you all… none of this would be possible.

Picture Credits

Chapter 1 - Dr. Sharon Zaffarese-Dippold, model Elijah Tubbs

Chapter 2 - Dr. Sharon Zaffarese-Dippold

Chapter 3 - Pdumond (Pixaby), https://pixabay.com/users/pdumond-180971/

Chapter 4 - Siggy Nowak (Brisbane, Australia) Pixaby, https://pixabay.com/photos/yacht-water-toy-boat-sailboat-499661/

Chapter 5 – Dr. Sharon Zaffarese-Dippold

Chapter 6 – Dr. Sharon Zaffarese Dippold

Chapter 7 - Pixaby-412Designs Image by https://pixabay.com/photos/dark-black-background-glass-3061610/

Chapter 8 - Congerdesign (Pixabay), https://pixabay.com/photos/goat-kid-cub-domestic-goat-food-490986/

Chapter 9 - *Picture Credit- @tawatchai07 (FreePix),* https://www.freepik.com/free-photo/girl-sitting-alone-wooden-bridge-sea-frustrated-depression_13181488.htm

Chapter 10 - Picture Credit (FreePix) https://www.freepik.com/free-photo/young-child-learning-how-play-electronic-keyboard_12259683.htm

Chapter 11 - @ededchechine (FreePix), https://www.freepik.com/free-photo/surf-pebble-beach-kumquat-carried-by-wave-beach-selective-focus-sea-bright-sunny-day-vacation-time-background-idea_40147177.htm

Chapter 12 - Dr. Sharon Zaffarese-Dippold, Dr. Sharon Zaffarese-Dippold with her brother, Carl.

Chapter 13 - Photo by Samantha Fortney on Unsplash

Chapter 14 – Dr. Sharon Zaffarese-Dippold, model Elijah Tubbs

Chapter 15 – FreePix, https://www.freepik.com/free-photo/cute-cat-lavender-field_29447615.htm

Chapter 16 - © Cheryl Casey | Dreamstime.com,

https://www.dreamstime.com/royalty-free-stock-image-girl-bear-window-image4533966

Chapter 17 - Created by Dr. Sharon Zaffarese-Dippold

Chapter 18 - Gabczi of Hungary, https://www.shutterstock.com/g/gabczi/about

Chapter 19 – THE Note, - Dr. Sharon Zaffarese-Dippold

Chapter 20 – Dr. Sharon Zaffarese-Dippold

Chapter 21 - <Dreamstime, https://www.dreamstime.com/group-friends-form-circle-lying-grass-hands-top-public-domain-image-free-117608524

Chapter 22 - -Pixabay Jimoody8 (Vincent Boulanger of France), https://pixabay.com/photos/wolves-park-wolf-wild-nature-3785362/